Internet of Things with ESP8266

Build amazing Internet of Things projects using the ESP8266 Wi-Fi chip

Marco Schwartz

PUBLISHING

BIRMINGHAM - MUMBAI

Internet of Things with ESP8266

Copyright © 2016 Packt Publishing

First published: July 2016

Production reference: 1260716

Published by Packt Publishing Ltd.
Livery Place
35 Livery Street
Birmingham B3 2PB, UK.

ISBN 978-1-78646-802-4

www.packtpub.com

Credits

Author
Marco Schwartz

Reviewer
Catalin Batrinu

Commissioning Editor
Pratik Shah

Acquisition Editor
Prachi Bisht

Content Development Editor
Mamta Walkar

Technical Editor
Naveenkumar Jain

Copy Editor
Sneha Singh

Project Coordinator
Kinjal Bari

Proofreader
Safis Editing

Indexer
Pratik Shirodkar

Graphics
Kirk D'Penha

Production Coordinator
Shantanu N. Zagade

Cover Work
Shantanu N. Zagade

About the Author

Marco Schwartz is an electrical engineer, an entrepreneur, and a blogger. He has a master's degree in electrical engineering and computer science from Supélec, France, and a master's degree in micro engineering from the Ecole Polytechnique Fédérale de Lausanne (EPFL) in Switzerland.

He has more than five years of experience working in the domain of electrical engineering. Marco's interests gravitate around electronics, home automation, the Arduino and Raspberry Pi platforms, open source hardware projects, and 3D printing.

He has several websites about Arduino, including the Open Home Automation website, which is dedicated to building home automation systems using open source hardware.

Marco has written another book on home automation and Arduino, called *Home Automation With Arduino: Automate Your Home Using Open-source Hardware*. He has also written a book on how to build Internet of Things projects with Arduino, called *Internet of Things with the Arduino Yun*, Packt Publishing.

About the Reviewer

Catalin Batrinu graduated from the Politehnica University of Bucharest in Electronics, Telecommunications and Information Technology. He has been working as a software developer in telecommunications for the past 16 years.

He has worked with old protocols and the latest network protocols and technologies, so he has seen all the transformations in the telecommunication industry.

He has implemented many telecommunications protocols, from access adaptations and backbone switches to high capacity, carrier-grade switches on various hardware platforms from Wintegra and Broadcom.

Internet of Things came as a natural evolution for him and now he collaborates with different companies to construct the world of tomorrow that will make our life more comfortable and secure.

Using ESP8266, he has prototyped devices such as irrigation controllers, smart sockets, window shutters, Digital Addressable Lighting Controls, and environment controls, all of them being controlled directly from a mobile application over the cloud. Even an MQTT broker with bridging and a websockets server was developed for the ESP8266. Soon, all those devices will be part of our daily life, so we will all enjoy their functionality.

You can read his blog at http://myesp8266.blogspot.com.

www.PacktPub.com

eBooks, discount offers, and more

Did you know that Packt offers eBook versions of every book published, with PDF and ePub files available? You can upgrade to the eBook version at www.PacktPub.com and as a print book customer, you are entitled to a discount on the eBook copy. Get in touch with us at customercare@packtpub.com for more details.

At www.PacktPub.com, you can also read a collection of free technical articles, sign up for a range of free newsletters and receive exclusive discounts and offers on Packt books and eBooks.

https://www2.packtpub.com/books/subscription/packtlib

Do you need instant solutions to your IT questions? PacktLib is Packt's online digital book library. Here, you can search, access, and read Packt's entire library of books.

Why subscribe?

- Fully searchable across every book published by Packt
- Copy and paste, print, and bookmark content
- On demand and accessible via a web browser

Table of Contents

Preface

The **Internet of Things (IoT)** is an exciting field that proposes to have all the devices that surround us connected to the Internet and interacting with us, but also between each other. It's estimated that there will be 50 billion IoT devices in the world by the year 2020.

On the other hand, the ESP8266 chip is a small, cheap (less than $5), and powerful Wi-Fi chip that is also really easy to program. Therefore, it is just the perfect tool to build inexpensive and nice IoT projects. In this book, you are going to learn everything you need to know on how to build IoT projects using the ESP8266 Wi-Fi chip.

What this book covers

Chapter 1, *Getting Started with the ESP8266*, will teach all you need to know about how to choose your ESP8266 board and upload your first sketch to the chip.

Chapter 2, *First Projects with the ESP8266*, will explain the basics of the ESP8266 by making some real simple projects.

Chapter 3, *Cloud Data Logging with the ESP8266*, will dive right into the core of the topic of the book, and build a project that can log measurement data on the cloud.

Chapter 4, *Control Devices from Anywhere*, will reveal how to control devices from anywhere in the world using the ESP8266.

Chapter 5, *Interacting With Web Services*, will show how to use the ESP8266 to interact with existing web platforms such as Twitter.

Chapter 6, Machine-to-Machine Communications, will explain how to make ESP8266 chips talk to each other via the cloud, to build applications that don't require human intervention.

Chapter 7, Sending Notifications from the ESP8266, will show how to send automated notifications from the ESP8266, for example, via text message or email.

Chapter 8, Controlling a Door Lock from the Cloud, will use what we learned so far in the book to build our first application: a door lock that can be controlled remotely.

Chapter 9, Building a Physical Bitcoin Ticker, will use the ESP8266 for a fun project: making a physical display of the current price of Bitcoin.

Chapter 10, Wireless Gardening with the ESP8266, will dive into a more complex, by learning how to automate your garden with the ESP8266.

Chapter 11, Cloud-Based Home Automation System, will show how to build the essential blocks of an home automation system using the ESP8266.

Chapter 12, Cloud-Controlled ESP8266 Robot, will explain how to use the ESP8266 to control a mobile robot from anywhere in the world.

Chapter 13, Building Your Own Cloud Platform to Control ESP8266 Devices, will reveal how to build our own cloud platform for your ESP8266 projects.

What you need for this book

For this book, you will need to have the Arduino IDE, which we will use for all the projects of the book. You will learn how to install it and configure it in the first chapter of the book.

The chapters of the book were also written with a progressive complexity, so even if you don't know a lot about Arduino and/or the ESP8266 you will be able to learn as you progress through the chapters. However, previous experience in programing (especially in C++ and/or JavaScript) is recommend for this book.

Who this book is for

This book is for those who want to build powerful and inexpensive IoT projects using the ESP8266 Wi-Fi chip, including those who are new to IoT, or those who already have experience with other platforms such as Arduino.

Conventions

In this book, you will find a number of text styles that distinguish between different kinds of information. Here are some examples of these styles and an explanation of their meaning.

Code words in text, database table names, folder names, filenames, file extensions, pathnames, dummy URLs, user input, and Twitter handles are shown as follows: "We can include other contexts through the use of the `include` directive."

A block of code is set as follows:

```
void loop() {
Serial.print("Connecting to ");
Serial.println(host);
// Use WiFiClient class to create TCP connections
WiFiClient client;
const int httpPort = 80;
if (!client.connect(host, httpPort)) {
Serial.println("connection failed");
return;
    }
```

Any command-line input or output is written as follows:

```
# cp /usr/src/asterisk-addons/configs/cdr_mysql.conf.sample
    /etc/asterisk/cdr_mysql.conf
```

New terms and **important words** are shown in bold. Words that you see on the screen, for example, in menus or dialog boxes, appear in the text like this: "Open **Boards Manager** from the **Tools | Board** menu and install the **esp8266** platform, as shown."

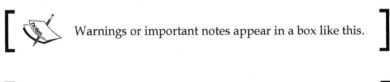

> Warnings or important notes appear in a box like this.

> Tips and tricks appear like this.

Reader feedback

Feedback from our readers is always welcome. Let us know what you think about this book—what you liked or disliked. Reader feedback is important for us as it helps us develop titles that you will really get the most out of.

To send us general feedback, simply e-mail feedback@packtpub.com, and mention the book's title in the subject of your message.

If there is a topic that you have expertise in and you are interested in either writing or contributing to a book, see our author guide at www.packtpub.com/authors.

Customer support

Now that you are the proud owner of a Packt book, we have a number of things to help you to get the most from your purchase.

Downloading the example code

You can download the example code files for this book from your account at http://www.packtpub.com. If you purchased this book elsewhere, you can visit http://www.packtpub.com/support and register to have the files e-mailed directly to you.

You can download the code files by following these steps:

1. Log in or register to our website using your e-mail address and password.
2. Hover the mouse pointer on the **SUPPORT** tab at the top.
3. Click on **Code Downloads & Errata**.
4. Enter the name of the book in the **Search** box.
5. Select the book for which you're looking to download the code files.
6. Choose from the drop-down menu where you purchased this book from.
7. Click on **Code Download**.

Once the file is downloaded, please make sure that you unzip or extract the folder using the latest version of:

- WinRAR / 7-Zip for Windows
- Zipeg / iZip / UnRarX for Mac
- 7-Zip / PeaZip for Linux

Downloading the color images of this book

We also provide you with a PDF file that has color images of the screenshots/ diagrams used in this book. The color images will help you better understand the changes in the output. You can download this file from `http://www.packtpub.com/ sites/default/files/downloads/InternetofThingswithESP8266_ ColorImages.pdf`.

Errata

Although we have taken every care to ensure the accuracy of our content, mistakes do happen. If you find a mistake in one of our books—maybe a mistake in the text or the code—we would be grateful if you could report this to us. By doing so, you can save other readers from frustration and help us improve subsequent versions of this book. If you find any errata, please report them by visiting `http://www.packtpub. com/submit-errata`, selecting your book, clicking on the **Errata Submission Form** link, and entering the details of your errata. Once your errata are verified, your submission will be accepted and the errata will be uploaded to our website or added to any list of existing errata under the Errata section of that title.

To view the previously submitted errata, go to `https://www.packtpub.com/books/ content/support` and enter the name of the book in the search field. The required information will appear under the **Errata** section.

Piracy

Piracy of copyrighted material on the Internet is an ongoing problem across all media. At Packt, we take the protection of our copyright and licenses very seriously. If you come across any illegal copies of our works in any form on the Internet, please provide us with the location address or website name immediately so that we can pursue a remedy.

Please contact us at `copyright@packtpub.com` with a link to the suspected pirated material.

We appreciate your help in protecting our authors and our ability to bring you valuable content.

Questions

If you have a problem with any aspect of this book, you can contact us at `questions@packtpub.com`, and we will do our best to address the problem.

1
Getting Started with the ESP8266

In this chapter, we are going to start by setting up the ESP8266 chip. We will learn how to choose the right module for your project and get all the additional hardware you need to use the chip. We will also see how to connect the ESP8266 to your computer, so you can program it using a USB cable.

Then, we are going to see how to configure and upload code to the ESP8266 chip. For that, we will be using the Arduino IDE. This makes using the ESP8266 much easier, as we will be using a well-known interface and language to configure the chip. We will also be able to use most of the already existing Arduino libraries for our projects. Let's start!

How to choose your ESP8266 module
We are first going to see how to choose the right ESP8266 module for your project. There are many modules available in the market and it is quite easy to get lost with all the choices available.

The first one that you have probably heard of is the small ESP8266 Serial Wireless Transceiver module:

This module is the most famous one, as it is really small and only costs $5. However, the number of accessible GPIO pins (input/output pins) is quite limited. It is also difficult to plug it into a standard breadboard.

If you choose this module, there are some projects in this book that you might not be able to do. For example, you won't be able to do the projects using analog sensors, as the analog input pin is not accessible.

You can find more information about this module at:

`https://nurdspace.nl/images/e/e0/ESP8266_Specifications_English.pdf`

But there are many other modules on the market that give you access to all the pins of the ESP8266. For example, I really like the ESP8266 Olimex module, which is also cheap (around $10):

This module can easily be mounted on a breadboard and you can easily access all the pins of the ESP8266. This is the one I will use for most of this book and therefore I also recommend that you use a similar module.

You can find additional details about this module at:

`https://www.olimex.com/Products/IoT/MOD-WIFI-ESP8266-DEV/open-source-hardware`

One other choice is to use a board based on the ESP-12, which is a version of the ESP8266 made to be integrated on PCBs. This version also gives you access to all the pins of the ESP8266. It is relatively easy to find breakout boards for this chip. For example, this is a board that I bought on Tindie:

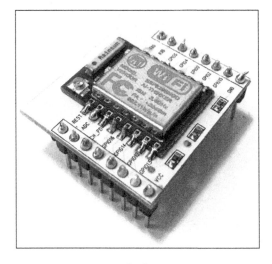

You can find more information about this module on:

http://www.seeedstudio.com/wiki/images/7/7d/ESP-12E_brief_spec.pdf

You can also get your hands on the Adafruit ESP8266 breakout board, which also integrates the ESP-12:

http://www.adafruit.com/product/2471

Another solution is to use the NodeMCU development kit, which is similar to the Olimex board but also has an integrated USB-to-Serial converter, as well as an onboard power supply. It is easier to use, but was hard to find at the time this book was written. You can get more information on the NodeMCU website:

http://nodemcu.com/index_en.html

Note that with the NodeMCU module, you will have to translate the pins from the module to the pins defined in the ESP8266 Arduino IDE, which we are going to use. You will find the correspondence between pins here:

https://github.com/nodemcu/nodemcu-firmware/wiki/nodemcu_api_en#new_gpio_map

Hardware requirements

Let's now take a look at the things we need to make the ESP8266 chip work. It is usually, but incorrectly, assumed that you just need this little chip and nothing else to make it work, but we are going to see that it is not true.

First, you will need some way to program the ESP8266. You can use an Arduino board for that, but for me the really great thing about the ESP8266 is that it can function completely autonomously, using the onboard processor.

So to program the chip, I will use a USB FTDI programmer.

 Note that it has to be compatible with the logic level of the ESP8266 chip, so 3.3V.

I have used a module that can be switched between 3.3V and 5V:

You will also need a dedicated power supply to power the chip. This is a point that is often forgotten and leads to a lot of issues. If you are, for example, trying to power the ESP8266 chip from the 3.3V coming from the FTDI board or from an Arduino board, it simply won't work correctly.

Therefore, for most ESP8266 modules, you need a dedicated power supply that can deliver at least 300 mA to be safe. Some boards have an integrated micro-USB port and a voltage regulator that can provide the required current to the ESP8266, but that's not the case with the board we will use in this first chapter. I used a breadboard power supply that can deliver up to 500 mA at 3.3V:

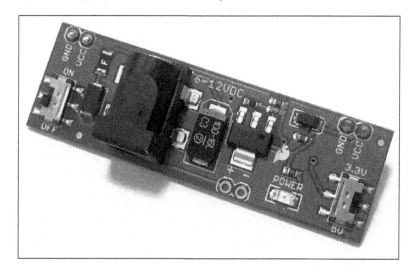

This is a list of all the components that you will need to use the ESP8266 chip:

- ESP8266 Olimex module (https://www.olimex.com/Products/IoT/MOD-WIFI-ESP8266-DEV/open-source-hardware)
- Breadboard 3.3V power supply (https://www.sparkfun.com/products/13032)
- 3.3V FTDI USB module (https://www.sparkfun.com/products/9873)
- Breadboard (https://www.sparkfun.com/products/12002)
- Jumper wires (https://www.sparkfun.com/products/12795)

Hardware configuration

We are now going to take a look at the way to configure the hardware for the first use of your ESP8266 board. This is how we connect the different components:

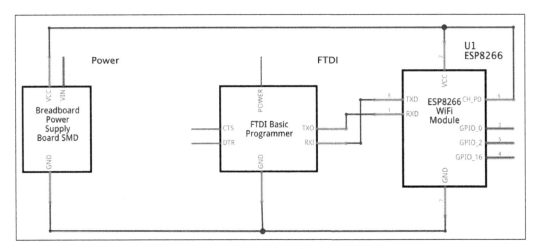

Depending on the board you are using, the pins can have different names. Therefore, I created pictures to help you out with each module. These are the pins you will need on the small ESP board:

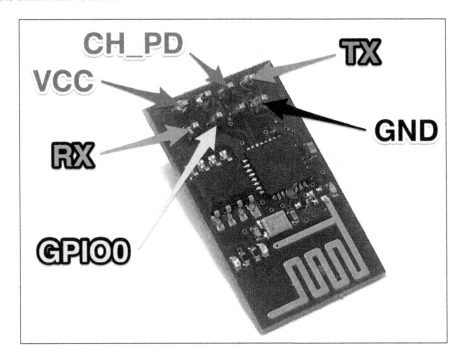

This is the same for the ESP-12 board mounted on a breadboard adapter:

Finally, this is the picture for the Olimex board:

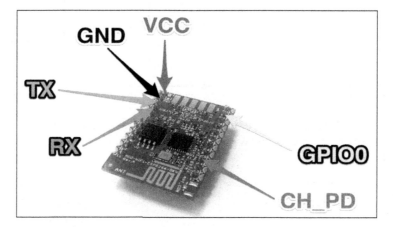

This is what the Olimex board will look like at the end:

Make sure that you connect everything according to the schematics or you won't be able to continue.

 Also, make sure that all the switches of your components (FTDI module and power supply) are set to 3.3V, or it will damage your chip.

Also, connect one wire to the GPIO 0 pin of the ESP8266. Don't connect it to anything else for now, but you will need it later to put the chip in programming mode.

Installing the Arduino IDE for the ESP8266

Now that we have completely set up the hardware for the ESP8266, we are ready to configure it using the Arduino IDE.

The most basic way to use the ESP8266 module is to use serial commands, as the chip is basically a Wi-Fi/Serial transceiver. However, this is not convenient and this is not what I recommend doing.

What I recommend is simply using the Arduino IDE, which you will need to install on your computer. This makes it very convenient to use the ESP8266 chip, as we will be using the well-known Arduino IDE, so this is the method that we will use in the entire book.

We are now going to configure your ESP8266 chip using the Arduino IDE. This is a great way to use the chip, as you will be able to program it using the well-known Arduino IDE and also re-use several existing Arduino libraries.

If this is not done yet, install the latest version of the Arduino IDE. You can get it from `http://www.arduino.cc/en/main/software`.

Now, you need to take a follow steps to be able to configure the ESP8266 with the Arduino IDE:

1. Start the **Arduino IDE** and open the **Preferences** window.

2. Enter the following URL into the **Additional Board Manager** URLs field:
    `http://arduino.esp8266.com/stable/package_esp8266com_index.json`

3. Open **Boards Manager** from the **Tools | Board** menu and install the **esp8266** platform as shown here:

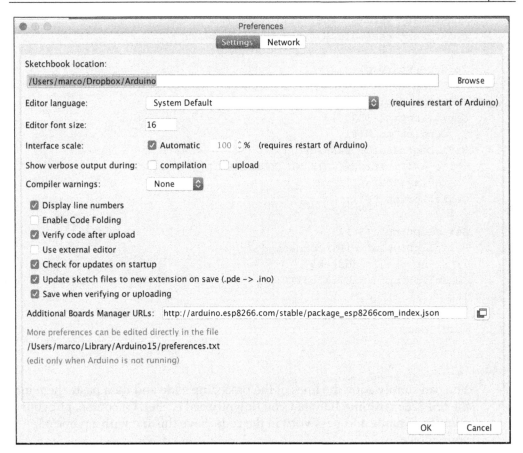

Connecting your module to your Wi-Fi network

Now, we are going to check whether the ESP8266 and the Arduino IDE are working correctly, and connect your chip to your local Wi-Fi network.

To do so, let's perform the following steps:

1. First, we need to write the code and then upload it to the board. The code is simple; we just want to connect to the local Wi-Fi network and print the IP address of the board. This is the code to connect to the network:

```
// Import required libraries
#include <ESP8266WiFi.h>

// WiFi parameters
```

```
constchar* ssid = "your_wifi_name";
constchar* password = "your_wifi_password";

void setup(void)
{
// Start Serial
Serial.begin(115200);
// Connect to WiFi
WiFi.begin(ssid, password);
while (WiFi.status() != WL_CONNECTED) {
    delay(500);
Serial.print(".");
  }
Serial.println("");
Serial.println("WiFi connected");
// Print the IP address
Serial.println(WiFi.localIP());
}

void loop() {

}
```

You can simply copy the lines of the preceding code and then paste them into the ESP8266 Arduino IDE that you downloaded earlier. Of course, put your own Wi-Fi name and password in the code. Save this file with a name of your choice.

2. Now, navigate to **Tools | Boards** and select **Generic ESP8266 Module**. Also, select the correct **Serial port** that corresponds to the FTDI converter that your are using.

3. After that, we need to put the board in the bootloader mode, so we can program it. To do so, connect the pin GPIO 0 to the ground, via the cable we plugged into GPIO 0. Then, power cycle the board by switching the power supply off and then on again.

4. Now, upload the code to the board and open the Serial monitor when this is done. Set the Serial monitor speed to **115200**. Now, disconnect the cable between GPIO 0 and GND and power cycle the board again. You should see the following message:

WiFi connected

192.168.1.103

If you can see this message and an IP, congratulations, your board is now connected to your Wi-Fi network! You are now ready to build your first projects using the ESP8266 chip.

Summary

In this first chapter of the book, we learned the fundamentals about the ESP8266. We first learned about all the different boards that are available for your ESP8266 projects. Then, we saw how to wire your ESP8266 modules. Finally, we saw how to install the Arduino IDE and to configure it for the ESP8266, and we ended the chapter by actually uploading a very simple sketch to the ESP8266.

In the next chapter, we are going to use the tools we set up and build some basic projects using the ESP8266 Wi-Fi chip.

2
First Projects with the ESP8266

Now that your ESP8266 chip is ready to be used and you can connect it to your Wi-Fi network, we can build some basic projects with it. This will help you understand the basics of the ESP8266.

We are going to see three projects in this chapter: how to control an LED, how to read data from a GPIO pin, and how to grab the contents from a web page. We will also see how to read data from a digital sensor.

Controlling an LED

First, we are going to see how to control a simple LED. The GPIO pins of the ESP8266 can be configured to realize many functions: inputs, outputs, PWM outputs, and also SPI or I2C communications. This first project will teach you how to use the GPIO pins of the chip as outputs:

1. The first step is to add an LED to our project. These are the extra components you will need for this project:

    ° 5 mm LED (`https://www.sparkfun.com/products/9590`)

    ° 330 Ohm resistor to limit the current in the LED (`https://www.sparkfun.com/products/8377`)

2. The next step is to connect the LED with the resistor to the ESP8266 board. To do so, the first thing to do is to place the resistor on the breadboard.

3. Then, place the LED on the breadboard as well, connecting the longest pin of the LED (the anode) to one pin of the resistor.

4. Then, connect the other end of the resistor to GPIO pin 5 of the ESP8266, and the other end of the LED to the ground.

This is what it should look like at the end:

5. We are now going to light up the LED by programming the ESP8266 chip, just as we did in the first chapter of the book by connecting it to the Wi-Fi network.

This is the complete code for this section:

```
// Import required libraries
#include <ESP8266WiFi.h>

void setup() {

// Set GPIO 5 as output
pinMode(5, OUTPUT);

// Set GPIO 5 on a HIGH state
digitalWrite(5, HIGH);

}
void loop() {

}
```

This code simply sets the GPIO pin as an output, and then applies a HIGH state to it. The HIGH state means that the pin is active, and that positive voltage (3.3V) is applied to the pin. A LOW state would mean that the output is at 0V.

6. You can now copy this code and paste it into the Arduino IDE.

7. Then, upload the code to the board, using the instructions from the previous chapter. You should immediately see that the LED lights up. You can shut it down again by using `digitalWrite(5, LOW)` in the code. You could also, for example, modify the code so the ESP8266 switches the LED on and off every second.

Reading data from a GPIO pin

In the second project in this chapter, we are going to read the state of a GPIO pin. For this, we will use the same pin as in the previous project. You can therefore remove the LED and the resistor that we used in the previous project.

Now, simply connect this pin (GPIO 5) of the board to the positive power supply on your breadboard with a wire, applying a 3.3V signal on this pin.

Reading data from a pin is really simple. This is the complete code for this part:

```
// Import required libraries
#include <ESP8266WiFi.h>

void setup(void)
{
// Start Serial (to display results on the Serial monitor)
Serial.begin(115200);

// Set GPIO 5 as input
pinMode(5, INPUT);}
void loop() {

// Read GPIO 5 and print it on Serial port
Serial.print("State of GPIO 5: ");
Serial.println(digitalRead(5));

// Wait 1 second
  delay(1000);
}
```

We simply set the pin as an input, read the value of this pin, and print it out every second. Copy and paste this code into the Arduino IDE, then upload it to the board using the instructions from the previous chapter.

This is the result you should get in the Serial monitor:

```
State of GPIO 5: 1
```

We can see that the returned value is 1 (digital state HIGH), which is what we expected, because we connected the pin to the positive power supply. As a test, you can also connect the pin to the ground, and the state should go to 0.

Grabbing the content from a web page

As the last project in this chapter, we are finally going to use the Wi-Fi connection of the chip to grab the content of a page. We will simply use the www.example.com page, as it's a basic page largely used for test purposes.

This is the complete code for this project:

```
// Import required libraries
#include <ESP8266WiFi.h>

// WiFi parameters
constchar* ssid = "your_wifi_network";
constchar* password = "your_wifi_password";

// Host
constchar* host = "www.example.com";

void setup() {
// Start Serial
Serial.begin(115200);

// We start by connecting to a WiFi network
Serial.println();
Serial.println();
Serial.print("Connecting to ");
Serial.println(ssid);
WiFi.begin(ssid, password);
while (WiFi.status() != WL_CONNECTED) {
    delay(500);
Serial.print(".");
  }
```

```
Serial.println("");
Serial.println("WiFi connected");
Serial.println("IP address: ");
Serial.println(WiFi.localIP());
}

int value = 0;

void loop() {

Serial.print("Connecting to ");
Serial.println(host);

// Use WiFiClient class to create TCP connections
WiFiClient client;
const int httpPort = 80;
if (!client.connect(host, httpPort)) {
Serial.println("connection failed");
return;
   }

// This will send the request to the server
client.print(String("GET /") + " HTTP/1.1\r\n" +
"Host: " + host + "\r\n" + "Connection: close\r\n\r\n");
  delay(10);

// Read all the lines of the reply from server and print them to
Serial
while(client.available()){
    String line = client.readStringUntil('\r');
Serial.print(line);
  }

Serial.println();
Serial.println("closing connection");
  delay(5000);

}
```

The code is really basic: we first open a connection to the example.com website, and then send a GET request to grab the content of the page. Using the while(client. available()) code, we also listen for incoming data, and print it all inside the Serial monitor.

You can now copy this code and paste it into the Arduino IDE. Then, upload it to the board using the instructions from *Chapter 1, Getting Started with the ESP8266*, in the section *Connecting Your Module to Your Wi-Fi Network*. This is what you should see in the Serial monitor:

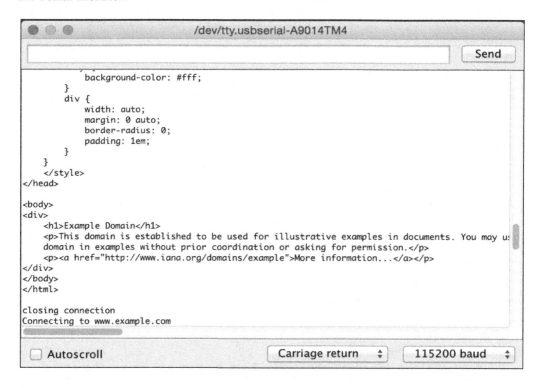

This is basically the content of the page, in pure HTML code.

Reading data from a digital sensor

In this last section of this chapter, we are going to connect a digital sensor to our ESP8266 chip, and read data from it. As an example, we will use a DHT11 sensor, which can be used to get ambient temperature and humidity.

You will need to get this component for this section, the DHT11 sensor (https://www.adafruit.com/products/386)

Let's now connect this sensor to your ESP8266:

1. First, place the sensor on the breadboard. Then, connect the first pin of the sensor to VCC, the second pin to pin 5 of the ESP8266, and the fourth pin of the sensor to GND.

   This is what it will look like at the end:

 Note that here I've used another ESP8266 board, the Adafruit ESP8266 breakout board. I will use this board in several chapters of this book.

We will also use the aREST framework in this example, so it's easy for you to access the measurements remotely. aREST is a complete framework to control your ESP8266 boards remotely (including from the cloud), and we are going to use it several times in the book. You can find more information about it at the following URL: http://arest.io/.

2. Let's now configure the board. The code is too long to be inserted here, but I will detail the most important part of it now.

 Note that you can find the code on the GitHub repository of the book: https://github.com/openhomeautomation/iot-esp8266-packt.

3. It starts by including the required libraries:

```
#include "ESP8266WiFi.h"
#include <aREST.h>
#include "DHT.h"
```

4. To install those libraries, simply look for them inside the Arduino IDE library manager. Next, we need to set the pin that the DHT sensor is connected to:

```
#define DHTPIN 5
#define DHTTYPE DHT11
```

5. After that, we declare an instance of the DHT sensor:

```
DHT dht(DHTPIN, DHTTYPE, 15);
```

6. As earlier, you will need to insert your own Wi-Fi name and password into the code:

```
const char* ssid = "wifi-name";
const char* password = "wifi-pass";
```

7. We also define two variables that will hold the measurements of the sensor:

```
float temperature;
float humidity;
```

8. In the `setup()` function of the sketch, we initialize the sensor:

```
dht.begin();
```

9. Still in the `setup()` function, we expose the variables to the aREST API, so we can access them remotely via Wi-Fi:

```
rest.variable("temperature", &temperature);
rest.variable("humidity", &humidity);
```

10. Finally, in the `loop()` function, we make the measurements from the sensor:

```
humidity = dht.readHumidity();
temperature = dht.readTemperature();
```

11. It's now time to test the project! Simply grab all the code and put it inside the Arduino IDE. Also make sure to install the aREST Arduino library using the Arduino library manager.

12. Now, put the ESP8266 board in bootloader mode, and upload the code to the board. After that, reset the board, and open the Serial monitor. You should see the IP address of the board being displayed:

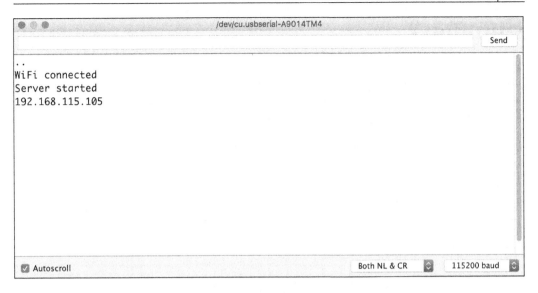

13. Now, we can access the measurements from the sensor remotely. Simply go to your favorite web browser, and type:

    ```
    192.168.115.105/temperature
    ```

    You should immediately get the answer from the board, with the temperature being displayed:

    ```
    {
      "temperature": 25.00,
    "id": "1",
    "name": "esp8266",
    "connected": true
    }
    ```

    You can of course do the same with humidity.

> Note that here we used the aREST API, which we will use in several other chapters in this book. You can learn more about it at http://arest.io/.

Congratulations, you just completed your very first projects using the ESP8266 chip! Feel free to experiment with what you learned in this chapter, and start learning more about how to configure your ESP8266 chip.

Summary

In this chapter, we realized our first basic projects using the ESP8266 Wi-Fi chip. We first learned how to control a simple output, by controlling the state of an LED. Then, we saw how to read the state of a digital pin on the chip. Finally, we learned how to read data from a digital sensor, and actually grab this data using the aREST framework which we will use in several chapters of this book.

In the next chapter, we are going to go right into the main topic of the book, and build our first Internet of Things project using the ESP8266.

3

Cloud Data Logging with the ESP8266

In this chapter, we are going to use the ESP8266 to automatically log temperature and humidity measurements in the cloud, and display these measurements inside an online dashboard.

By following this project, you will be able to build a small and cheap measurement platform that logs data in the cloud. Of course, this can be applied to several types of sensor, such as motion detectors. Let's dive in!

Hardware and software requirements

For this project, you will need the following hardware:

- Of course you need an ESP8266 chip. You can, for example, use an Olimex ESP8266 module.

- You will also need a temperature sensor. I used a DHT11 sensor, which is very easy to use and will allow us to measure the ambient temperature and humidity.

- You will also need a 3.3V FTDI USB module to program the ESP8266 chip. Finally, you will also need some jumper wires and a breadboard.

This is a list of all the components that will be used in this chapter, along with the sources where you can purchase them:

- ESP8266 Olimex module (`https://www.olimex.com/Products/IoT/MOD-WIFI-ESP8266-DEV/open-source-hardware`)
- Breadboard 3.3V power supply (`https://www.sparkfun.com/products/13032`)
- 3.3V FTDI USB module (`https://www.sparkfun.com/products/9873`)
- DHT11 sensor (`https://www.adafruit.com/products/386`)
- Breadboard (`https://www.sparkfun.com/products/12002`)
- Jumper wires (`https://www.sparkfun.com/products/9194`)

On the software side, you will need:

- The latest version of the Arduino IDE, which you can get from: `http://www.arduino.cc/en/Main/Software`.

Now let's follow this procedure to add the ESP8266 board to the Arduino IDE:

1. Start the Arduino IDE and open the **Preferences** window.
2. Enter the following URL into the **Additional Board Manager URLs** field:

   `http://arduino.esp8266.com/package_esp8266com_index.json`

3. Open `Boards Manager` by navigating to the **Tools | Board** menu, and install the **esp8266 platform**.
4. You will also need the DHT library, which you can get from:

   `https://github.com/adafruit/DHT-sensor-library`

To install an Arduino library:

1. First, download the library from the GitHub repository.
2. Then, go into the Arduino IDE, and navigate to **Sketch | Include Library | Add .ZIP Library**.
3. Finally, select the file that you just downloaded.

Hardware configuration

We are first going to see how to configure the hardware to use the ESP8266 board. This is how to connect the different components:

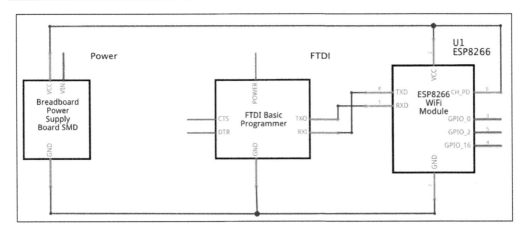

1. Basically, you need to connect your breadboard power supply VCC and GND to the ESP8266 VCC and GND. Also, connect the GND pin of the FTDI converter board to the ESP8266 GND.

2. Then, connect TX from the FTDI board to RX of the ESP8266 board, and then RX to TX.

3. Finally, connect the CH_PD (or CHIP_EN) pin of the ESP8266 board to VCC.

4. Once this is done, simply put the DHT11 sensor on the breadboard.

5. Then, connect the left pin to VCC (red power rail), the right pin to GND (blue power rail), and the pin next to VCC to the GPIO pin 5 on your ESP8266 chip. This is the final result, not showing the USB-to-Serial FTDI cables:

> Make sure that you've connected everything according to the schematics, or you won't be able to continue. Also make sure that all the switches of your components (FTDI module and power supply) are set to 3.3V, or it will damage your chip.

6. Also, connect one wire to GPIO pin 0 of the ESP8266. Don't connect it to anything else for now, but you will need it later to put the chip in programming mode.

Testing the sensor

We are now going to use the sensor. Again, remember that we are using the Arduino IDE, so we can code just like we would do using an Arduino board. Here, we will simply print the value of the temperature inside the Serial monitor of the Arduino IDE. If it has not been done yet, install the Adafruit DHT sensor library using the Arduino IDE library manager.

This is the complete code for this part:

```
// Libraries
#include "DHT.h"

// Pin
#define DHTPIN 5

// Use DHT11 sensor
#define DHTTYPE DHT11

// Initialize DHT sensor
DHT dht(DHTPIN, DHTTYPE, 15);

void setup() {

// Start Serial
Serial.begin(115200);

// Init DHT
dht.begin();
}

void loop() {
```

```
// Reading temperature and humidity
float h = dht.readHumidity();
// Read temperature as Celsius
float t = dht.readTemperature();

// Display data
Serial.print("Humidity: ");
Serial.print(h);
Serial.print(" %\t");
Serial.print("Temperature: ");
Serial.print(t);
Serial.println(" *C ");

// Wait 2 seconds between measurements.
delay(2000);


}
```

Let's see the details of the code. You can see that all the measurement part is contained inside the `loop()` function, which makes the code inside it repeat every 2 seconds.

Then, we read data from the DHT11 sensor, and print the value of the temperature and humidity on the Serial port.

Note that the complete code can also be found inside the GitHub repository for the project:

`https://github.com/openhomeautomation/iot-esp8266`

Now let's start with the steps to test the sensor:

1. Paste the previous code into the Arduino IDE. Then, go to **Tools | Boards**, and select **Generic ESP8266 Module**. Also select the correct Serial port that corresponds to the FTDI converter you are using.

2. After that, we need to put the board in bootloader mode, so we can program it. To do so, connect GPIO pin 0 to the ground, via the cable we plugged into GPIO 0 before.

3. Then, power cycle the board by switching the power supply off and then on again.

4. Now, upload the code to the board and open the Serial monitor when this is done. Also, set the Serial monitor speed to 115200.

5. Now, disconnect the cable between GPIO 0 and GND, and power cycle the board again.

You should immediately see the temperature and humidity readings inside the Serial monitor. My sensor was reading around 24 degrees Celsius when I tested it, which is a realistic value.

Logging data to Dweet.io

We are now going to see how to log the temperature and humidity measurements in the cloud. We will use the Dweet.io cloud service here, which is very convenient for logging data online:

```
http://dweet.io/
```

> As the code for this part is very long, we will only see the important parts here. You can of course get all the code from the GitHub repository for this project at `https://github.com/openhomeautomation/iot-esp8266`.

Again all the measurements are done inside the `loop()` function of the sketch, which makes the code repeat every 10 seconds, using a `delay()` function.

Inside this loop, we connect to the Dweet.io server with:

```
WiFiClient client;
const int httpPort = 80;
if (!client.connect(host, httpPort)) {
Serial.println("connection failed");
return;
}
```

Then, we read the data from the sensor with:

```
int h = dht.readHumidity();
int t = dht.readTemperature();
```

After that, we send data to the Dweet.io server with:

```
client.print(String("GET /dweet/for/myesp8266?temperature=") +
  String(t) + "&humidity=" + String(h) + " HTTP/1.1\r\n" +
"Host: " + host + "\r\n" +
"Connection: close\r\n\r\n");
```

You might want to replace `myesp8266` here, which is your device name on Dweet.io. Use a complicated name (just like a password) to make sure you are creating a unique device on Dweet.io.

We also print any data received on the serial port with:

```
while(client.available()){
   String line = client.readStringUntil('\r');
Serial.print(line);
}
```

 Note that you also need to modify the code to insert your own Wi-Fi network name and password. You can now upload the code to the ESP8266 board, using the instructions that we saw earlier, and open the Serial monitor.

You should see that every 10 seconds, the request is sent to the `Dweet.io server`, and you get the answer back:

```
HTTP/1.1 200 OK
Access-Control-Allow-Origin: *
Content-Type: application/json
Content-Length: 147
Date: Mon, 16 Mar 2015 10:03:37 GMT
Connection: keep-alive

{"this":"succeeded","by":"dweeting","the":"dweet",
"with":{"thing":"myesp8266","created":"2015-03-16T10:03:37.053Z",
"content":{"temperature":24, "humidity":39}
   }
}
```

If you can see the `succeeded` message, congratulations, you just logged data in the cloud with your ESP8266 chip!

Displaying data using Freeboard.io

Now, we would like to actually display the recorded data inside a dashboard that can be accessed from anywhere in the world. For that, we are going to use a service that I love to use along with Dweet.io: Freeboard.io.

Let's get started with using Freeboard.io:

1.   First, create an account there by going to:

     `https://www.freeboard.io/`

2.   Then, create a new dashboard, and inside this dashboard, create a new
     `datasource`. Link this `datasource` to your **Dweet.io** thing that you defined
     in the ESP8266 code:

3.   Now create a new Gauge widget that we will use to display the temperature.
     Give it a name, and link it to the temperature field of our datasource:

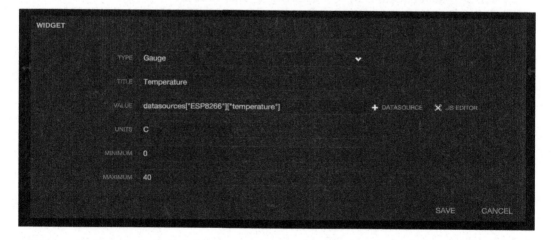

This is the final result:

You should see that the temperature data coming from the ESP8266 is logged every 10 seconds and is immediately displayed inside the Freeboard.io panel. Congratulations, you have built a very small and cheap and temperature sensor that logs data in the cloud!

You can then do the same with the humidity measurements and also display them on this dashboard:

It is also really easy to add other widgets to the dashboard. For example, you may want to plot the history of the temperature and humidity measurements. For that, there is a widget called Sparkline. You can create it just as you created the Gauge widget. Start with the temperature widget:

You can now do the same for the humidity:

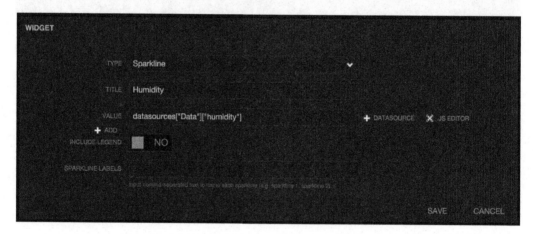

This is the final result inside the dashboard:

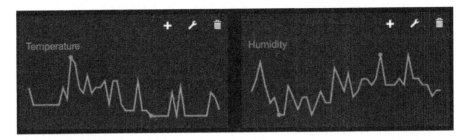

Summary

Let's summarize what we did in this project. We built a simple and cheap Wi-Fi temperature sensor based on the ESP8266 chip. We configured it to automatically log data on the Dweet.io service, and we displayed these measurements inside an online dashboard.

There are many ways to improve this project. You can simply add more sensors to the project, and display these measurements as well inside the Freeboard.io dashboard.

You can also, for example, completely change the project, by connecting a motion sensor to the ESP8266 board. You can then configure this sensor to automatically send you an alert when motion is detected, for example via e-mail or using Twitter. The possibilities are endless!

In the next chapter, we are going to see how to do another important thing in any IoT project: controlling devices from the cloud.

4
Control Devices from Anywhere

In the previous chapter, we saw how to make measurements with the ESP8266 chip, and send this data to the web. We saw how to log this data on the cloud, and display it inside a dashboard that can be accessed from anywhere.

In this chapter, we are going to see the reverse situation: how can we control devices from anywhere in the world? We will see that it requires using a different protocol than the classical HTTP, called MQTT.

MQTT can be difficult to use; this is why we will use a library that I created, called aREST, which will simplify the whole process. aREST only uses some of the powerful features of MQTT, but it will be more than enough here to control devices from anywhere.

We will see two examples in this chapter: how to dim an LED and how to control a lamp, both from anywhere in the world. We will see how to do that using a dashboard in the cloud.

At the end of this project, you will be able to control a lamp connected to your ESP8266 chip with a simple click on a dashboard that can be accessed from anywhere in the world. Let's dive in!

Hardware and software requirements

For this project, you will of course need an ESP8266 chip. As for most of this book, I used the Adafruit Huzzah ESP8266 module, but any ESP8266 module will work fine here.

You will also need some way to control your lamp or other devices. I originally used a simple relay for my tests, but I quickly moved to a PowerSwitch Tail Kit which allows you to simply and safely plug high voltage devices into your projects.

For the LED, I used a simple 5 mm red LED, along with a 330 Ohm resistor.

You will also need a 3.3V/5V FTDI USB module to program the ESP8266 chip.

Finally, you will also need some jumper wires and a breadboard.

This is a list of all the components, along with the web pages where you can find them, that will be used in this guide:

- Adafruit ES8266 module (https://www.adafruit.com/products/2471)
- FTDI USB module (https://www.adafruit.com/products/284)
- LED (https://www.sparkfun.com/products/9590)
- 330 Ohm resistor (https://www.sparkfun.com/products/8377)
- PowerSwitch Tail Kit (https://www.sparkfun.com/products/10747)
- Breadboard (https://www.sparkfun.com/products/12002)
- Jumper wires (https://www.sparkfun.com/products/9194)

 Note that you will also need a device to control. I used a simple 30 W desk lamp as a test device, but you can also use any other device in your home (if the power rating is lower than the maximum power accepted by the PowerSwitch Tail Kit). You could, for example, control a lamp, but also a coffee machine, a washing machine, an oven, and so on. You can also just use a simple relay or the LED for test purposes.

On the software side, if it's not done yet, you will need to install the latest version of the Arduino IDE, which you can get from:

http://www.arduino.cc/en/Main/Software

Then, you will also need to have the aREST and the PubSubClient libraries installed. To install a library, simply use the Arduino library manager.

You will also need to create an account on the aREST dashboard website:

`http://dashboard.arest.io/`

Configuring the ESP8266 module and controlling an LED

We are now going to configure the ESP8266 module, which means building the hardware and also configuring the board so it can receive commands from the cloud.

Simply place the ESP8266 board on your breadboard, and then connect the FTDI breakout board to it.

For the LED, simply connect it in series with the resistor, with the longest pin of the LED connected to the resistor. Then, connect the remaining pin of the resistor to pin 5 of the ESP8266 board, and the remaining pin of the LED to the GND pin.

This is the final result:

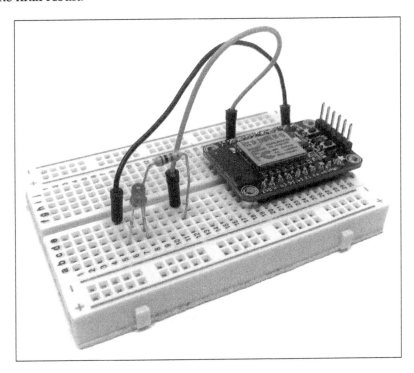

We are now going to configure the board so it can receive commands from the cloud.

This is the complete sketch for this part:

```
// Import required libraries
#include <ESP8266WiFi.h>
#include <PubSubClient.h>
#include <aREST.h>

// Clients
WiFiClient espClient;
PubSubClient client(espClient);

// Create aREST instance
aREST rest = aREST(client);

// Unique ID to identify the device for cloud.arest.io
char* device_id = "9u2co4";

// WiFi parameters
const char* ssid = "wifi-name";
const char* password = "wifi-password";

// Functions
void callback(char* topic, byte* payload, unsigned int length);

void setup(void)
{
  // Start Serial
  Serial.begin(115200);

  // Set callback
  client.setCallback(callback);

  // Give name and ID to device
  rest.set_id(device_id);
  rest.set_name("devices_control");

  // Connect to WiFi
  WiFi.begin(ssid, password);
  while (WiFi.status() != WL_CONNECTED) {
    delay(500);
    Serial.print(".");
  }
  Serial.println("");
```

```
    Serial.println("WiFi connected");

    // Set output topic
    char* out_topic = rest.get_topic();

}

void loop() {

    // Connect to the cloud
    rest.handle(client);

}

// Handles message arrived on subscribed topic(s)
void callback(char* topic, byte* payload, unsigned int length) {

    rest.handle_callback(client, topic, payload, length);

}
```

Let's now see this sketch in more detail.

It starts by including the required libraries:

```
#include <ESP8266WiFi.h>
#include <PubSubClient.h>
#include <aREST.h>
```

Then, we declare the Wi-Fi and PubSub clients:

```
WiFiClient espClient;
PubSubClient client(espClient);
```

After that, we create the aREST instance that will allow the board to process commands coming from the cloud:

```
aREST rest = aREST(client);
```

Let's now see two important points inside the sketch that you will need to modify for your own project.

The first one is the device ID:

```
char* device_id = "9u2co4";
```

Here, you really need to set you own ID, as this will identify the device on the network. There may be other people on the cloud server using the same ID, so make sure you are using something unique.

Then, set your Wi-Fi network name and password:

```
const char* ssid = "wifi-name";
const char* password = "wifi-password";
```

After that, inside the setup() function of the sketch, we set the callback. We'll see in a minute what this means, but for now we just pass it to the PubSubClient instance:

```
client.setCallback(callback);
```

Still in the setup() function, we set the device ID and name:

```
rest.set_id(device_id);
rest.set_name("devices_control");
```

In the loop() function of the sketch, we make sure the board always tries to connect to the cloud server with:

```
rest.handle(client);
```

Finally, we define the callback function. This will simply process the incoming requests from the cloud, and answer accordingly:

```
void callback(char* topic, byte* payload, unsigned int length) {

    rest.handle_callback(client, topic, payload, length);

}
```

It's now time to test our project! For now, we'll simply make sure that it is indeed connected to the cloud server.

First, upload the code to the board. Make sure that you modified the device ID and the Wi-Fi settings inside the code. To actually upload the code to the board, follow the instructions we saw in earlier chapters of this book.

All the requests to the board will now be done through the aREST cloud server, located at:

```
http://cloud.arest.io
```

To actually test it, go to your favorite web browser, and type:

```
http://cloud.arest.io/9u2co4/id
```

Of course, you need to replace the ID of the board with the one you set inside the sketch. This will basically check whether the board is online on the cloud server. If that's the case, you should get a similar answer in your web browser:

```
  {
"id": "9u2co4",
"name": "devices_control",
"connected": true
  }
```

This indicates that our device is now online and responding to the commands.

But let's not stop here; we are actually going to light up the LED from the cloud. First, we need to set pin 5 as an output. To do so, simply type:

```
https://cloud.arest.io/9u2co4/mode/5/o
```

You should receive the following message as a confirmation:

```
{
   "message": "Pin D5 set to output",
   "id": "9u2co4",
   "name": "devices_control",
   "connected": true
}
```

Then, turn the LED on with:

```
https://cloud.arest.io/9u2co4/digital/5/1
```

You should immediately see that the LED has turned on, and you should also receive the confirmation message in your browser:

```
{
   "message": "Pin D5 set to 1",
   "id": "9u2co4",
   "name": "devices_control",
   "connected": true
}
```

Congratulations, you can now control an LED from anywhere in the world! To learn more about aREST and the commands you can use, you can go to:

```
http://arest.io/
```

Controlling the LED from a cloud dashboard

It's nice to be able to control an LED from your web browser, but what we really want is to be able to control it from a nice graphical interface, from anywhere in the world.

This is exactly what we are going to do in this section, by using a service called the aREST dashboard. We will actually use it not only to control the LED, but also to dim the LED using a slider, right from your browser.

If it's not been done yet, create an account at:

`http://dashboard.arest.io/`

You should be able to create a new dashboard from the main interface:

Now, inside the dashboard, we are going to create a new element to control and dim the LED.

Create a dashboard element of the **Analog** type, and also insert the ID of the device you want to control. Also don't forget to set the pin to **5**:

You should instantly see the newly created element inside the dashboard:

Now, try the slider that you just created:

You should notice that whenever you move this slider and release the mouse, it should dim the LED accordingly. This is, for example, perfect for dimming an LED light that you have in your home.

Controlling the lamp from anywhere in the world

We are now going to use the same principles and code that we used so far for another application: controlling a lamp (or any electrical appliance) from anywhere in the world.

The configuration for this section is very simple: first, place the ESP8266 module on the breadboard, if that's not been done yet. Then, connect the Vin+ pin of the PowerSwitch Tail to the pin number 5 of the ESP8266. Finally, connect the two remaining pins of the PowerSwitch Tail to the GND pins of the ESP8266.

This is a picture of the final result:

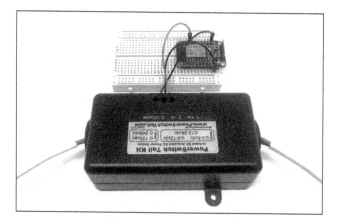

Then, connect the lamp (or the electrical appliance of your choosing) to the PowerSwitch Tail, and the other end of the PowerSwitch to the mains electricity.

For the code, simply use the exact same code as in the previous section: the main changes will only happen inside the dashboard itself.

Inside the dashboard, delete the previous slider element, and create a new one of the **Digital** type, using the same parameters as before:

You should see that the newly created element will immediately appear inside the dashboard:

You can now go ahead and test those buttons: you should notice that it immediately activates or deactivates the lamp or the device connected to the PowerSwitch.

As an illustration of the project in a real-life situation, here is a picture of the device we just created, connected to a desk lamp:

You can now control any electrical device from anywhere in the world, using the cloud dashboard that we used for this project.

Summary

Let's summarize what we achieved in this project. We used the MQTT protocol to control an LED, a lamp or any electrical devices from anywhere in the world, via the ESP8266 Wi-Fi chip. We configured the ESP8266 as an MQTT client, and then connected to the aREST dashboard so we could control it from anywhere we are in the world.

There are many things you can do to improve this project. You can, for example, add more modules like this one to your aREST dashboard, to control all the lamps inside your home remotely. You can also add other devices, such as sensors, to your dashboard, which is what we will see later in this book.

In the next chapter, we are going to look at another very important topic in the Internet of Things: how to make our ESP8266 devices interact with web services such as Facebook or Twitter.

5

Interacting With Web Services

In this book so far, we have seen how to monitor and control our ESP8266 Wi-Fi module from anywhere in the world. However, that's only a small part of what we can do within the Internet of Things framework.

What we will do in this chapter is use the ESP8266 to interact with existing web services, and therefore make the physical world interact with those services via the ESP8266. As examples, we'll connect the chip to the Yahoo Weather service, and then to Twitter and Facebook. Let's start!

Hardware and software requirements

For this project, you will of course need an ESP8266 chip. As for most of this book, I used the Adafruit Huzzah ESP8266 module, but any ESP8266 module will work fine here.

At some point, we will also tweet data on Twitter via the ESP8266. For that, I will use a simple DHT11 temperature and humidity sensor. Of course, you could easily use another sensor for this task.

Finally, you will also need some jumper wires and a breadboard.

This is a list of all the components that will be used in this guide:

- Adafruit ES8266 module (https://www.adafruit.com/products/2471)
- FTDI USB module (https://www.adafruit.com/products/284)
- DHT11 sensor (https://www.adafruit.com/products/386)
- Breadboard (https://www.sparkfun.com/products/12002)
- Jumper wires (https://www.sparkfun.com/products/9194)

On the software side, if it's not been done yet, you will need to install the latest version of the Arduino IDE, which you can get from here:

```
http://www.arduino.cc/en/Main/Software
```

You will also need to create an account on the **Temboo** website. We will use **Temboo** to interface the ESP8266 with web services such as Yahoo or Twitter. First, create an account on the **Temboo** website:

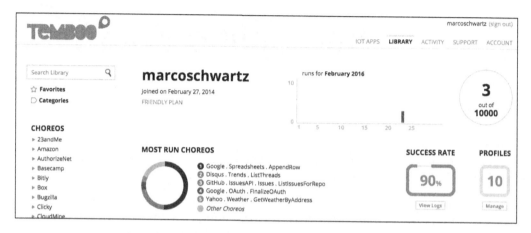

After that, go to **Account** and create a first application. You will need the app name and key later in this chapter:

You will also need to have a custom version of the Temboo library that I modified to work with the ESP8266. You can find it inside the code for this chapter, which you can find inside the GitHub repository for the book:

```
https://github.com/openhomeautomation/iot-esp8266-packt
```

Then, go to the **Arduino** main library folder (for Windows, under `C:\Program Files (x86)\Arduino\libraries`; for OS X, click on **Show package content** on the Arduino application). Make sure to save the existing `Temboo` library so you can reuse it later for projects other than the ESP9266. After that, delete the existing `Temboo` library and replace it with the one you got from the code for this chapter.

Getting weather data from Yahoo

For the first project in this chapter, we are actually going to learn how to grab weather data from the Yahoo Weather service. We'll see that it is really easy thanks to Temboo:

1. First, go to the following URL:

    `https://temboo.com/library/Library/Yahoo/Weather/`
    `GetWeatherByAddress/`

2. As it's your first time using Temboo, you will need to create a new "shield" for the Temboo service. Don't worry, I know we are not using an Arduino shield here; at the time this book was written, Temboo just didn't support the ESP8266 Wi-Fi chip.

    The best we can do is to select the Wi-Fi shield for Arduino, which is very close in terms of software. Inside the same screen, also enter your own Wi-Fi network SSID and password:

This will allow you to not have to re-enter those parameters every time. You should now see your newly created shield on the same page:

Now, we are going to see how to automatically generate the code for our project. We'll then just need to slightly modify it for our needs.

3. Now indicate your city inside the Temboo interface:

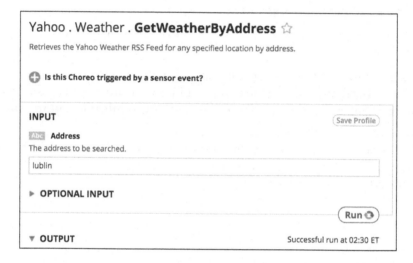

4. Then, you can either test it by clicking on **Run**, or generate the code:

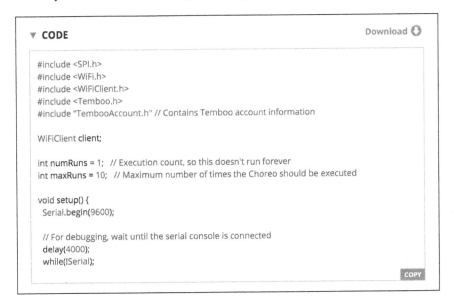

5. Now, download the code and place it inside a folder on your computer. You can either use this code, or simply get the code for this chapter.

6. We are now going to see the details of this code. There are actually only two lines you need to change if you want to use this sketch with the ESP8266. You need to change the Wi-Fi and Wi-Fi client libraries for the ESP8266WiFi library:

```
#include <SPI.h>
#include <ESP8266WiFi.h>
#include <Temboo.h>
#include "TembooAccount.h" // Contains Temboo account information
```

Then, we define how many times we want to run this code (Temboo is paid after a number of calls):

```
int numRuns = 1;    // Execution count, so this doesn't run forever
int maxRuns = 10;   // Maximum number of times the Choreo should
be executed
```

7. Inside the `setup()` function of the sketch, we connect the board to the Wi-Fi network:

```
int wifiStatus = WL_IDLE_STATUS;

// Determine if the WiFi Shield is present
Serial.print("\n\nShield:");
if (WiFi.status() == WL_NO_SHIELD) {
  Serial.println("FAIL");

  // If there's no WiFi shield, stop here
  while(true);
}

Serial.println("OK");

// Try to connect to the local WiFi network
while(wifiStatus != WL_CONNECTED) {
  Serial.print("WiFi:");
  wifiStatus = WiFi.begin(WIFI_SSID, WPA_PASSWORD);

  if (wifiStatus == WL_CONNECTED) {
    Serial.println("OK");
  } else {
    Serial.println("FAIL");
  }
  delay(5000);
}

Serial.println("Setup complete.\n");
}
```

8. Then, in the `loop()` function of the sketch, we send the request to Temboo, and we print the result inside the **Serial** monitor:

```
if (numRuns <= maxRuns) {
  Serial.println("Running GetWeatherByAddress - Run #" +
String(numRuns++));

  TembooChoreo GetWeatherByAddressChoreo(client);
```

```
  // Invoke the Temboo client
  GetWeatherByAddressChoreo.begin();

  // Set Temboo account credentials
  GetWeatherByAddressChoreo.setAccountName(TEMBOO_ACCOUNT);
  GetWeatherByAddressChoreo.setAppKeyName(TEMBOO_APP_KEY_NAME);
  GetWeatherByAddressChoreo.setAppKey(TEMBOO_APP_KEY);

  // Set Choreo inputs
  String AddressValue = "lublin";
  GetWeatherByAddressChoreo.addInput("Address", AddressValue);

  // Identify the Choreo to run
  GetWeatherByAddressChoreo.setChoreo("/Library/Yahoo/Weather/
GetWeatherByAddress");

  // Run the Choreo; when results are available, print them to
serial
  GetWeatherByAddressChoreo.run();

  while(GetWeatherByAddressChoreo.available()) {
    char c = GetWeatherByAddressChoreo.read();
    Serial.print(c);
  }
  GetWeatherByAddressChoreo.close();
  }

  Serial.println("\nWaiting...\n");
  delay(30000); // wait 30 seconds between GetWeatherByAddress
calls
```

9. It's now time to test this first project of the chapter! Simply check inside Temboo.h that all the parameters are correct, put the board into bootloader mode (so it can be programmed), and then upload the code to the board.

10. After that, open the Serial monitor. You should see that the board is grabbing data from the Yahoo Weather service, and displaying it inside the Serial monitor:

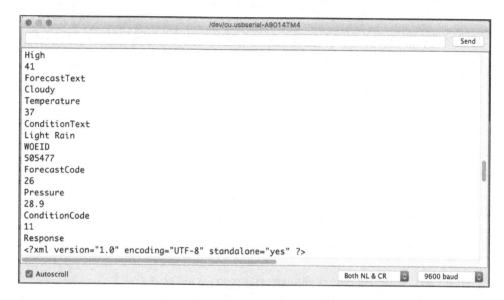

You can check the local temperature, humidity, and other weather data right from your ESP8266!

Posting temperature and humidity data to Twitter

In this second project of the chapter, we are going to see how to actually post measured data on your Twitter account.

We first need to configure the ESP8266 module, which means building the hardware with the DHT11 sensor.

Simply place the ESP8266 board on your breadboard, and then place the DHT11 sensor next to it. Connect the first pin of the DHT11 sensor to the VCC pin of the ESP8266, the second pin to pin 5 of the ESP board, and finally the last pin of the sensor to one GND pin of the ESP board.

This the final result:

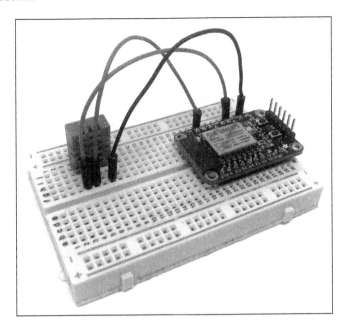

1. Now, we need to register an application with Twitter before we can create new tweets with our data. To do that, go over to:

    `https://apps.twitter.com/`

    You will be asked to log in with your Twitter account. Then, you can see your existing apps if you have some:

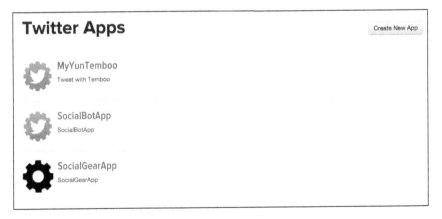

2. Click on the **CreateNew App** button, and give it a name and a default URL (this doesn't matter):

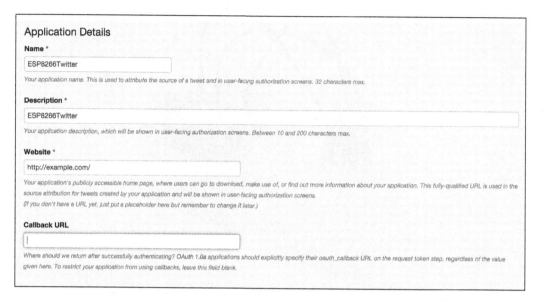

Once it's created, you will be able to access important parameters, such as the consumer key:

Application Settings

Your application's Consumer Key and Secret are used to **authenticate** *requests to the Twitter Platform.*

Access level   Read and write (modify app permissions)

Consumer Key (API Key)   (manage keys and access tokens)

On the settings tab, you will also be able to see the API secret key:

Application Settings

Keep the "Consumer Secret" a secret. This key should never be human-readable in your application.

Consumer Key (API Key)	
Consumer Secret (API Secret)	
Access Level	Read and write (modify app permissions)
Owner	MarcoSchwartz
Owner ID	

3. Then, on the same page, create a token for the application:

Your Access Token

This access token can be used to make API requests on your own account's behalf. Do not share your access token secret with anyone.

Access Token	
Access Token Secret	
Access Level	Read and write
Owner	MarcoSchwartz
Owner ID	81862926

This will give you an access token and a token secret. You will need those four to configure the project in Temboo.

4. Now, go to:

```
https://temboo.com/library/Library/Twitter/Tweets/
StatusesUpdate/
```

You will be able to fill in the four parameters from the Twitter app:

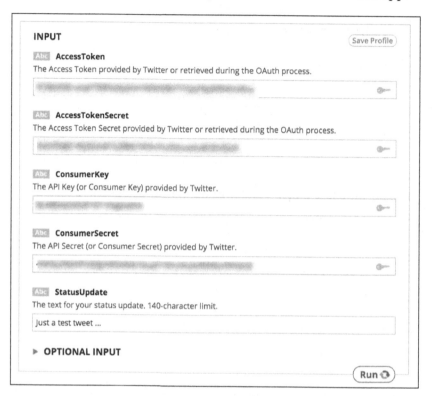

5. After that, generate the code for the sketch again. Don't worry about the content of the status update; we will change it later.

6. As before, you just need to modify the sketch a bit, so include the ESP8266WiFi library and insert the DHT library:

```
#include <SPI.h>
#include <ESP8266WiFi.h>
#include <Temboo.h>
#include "TembooAccount.h" // Contains Temboo account information
#include "DHT.h"
```

7. After that, we insert the code for the DHT11 sensor:

```
// DHT11 sensor pins
#define DHTPIN 5
#define DHTTYPE DHT11

// Initialize DHT sensor with the correct option for the ESP8266
DHT dht(DHTPIN, DHTTYPE, 15);
```

8. Inside the `setup()` function, we need to initialize the DHT11 sensor:

```
// Init DHT
dht.begin();
```

9. Then, inside the `loop()` function, the only thing we need to add is the code to read data from the sensor:

```
// Read data
float h = dht.readHumidity();
float t = dht.readTemperature();
```

10. We also need to modify the value of the status update string, to insert the measurements made by the sensor:

```
String StatusUpdateValue = "The temperature is " + String(t) + "
and the humidity is " + String(h) + ".";
```

11. It's finally time to test the sketch! Check the parameters inside the `Temboo.h` file, and after that upload the code to the ESP8266 board.

After a while, you should see that a new tweet was posted on your account, along with the data from the sensor:

Congratulations, you can now post data from your ESP8266 to a Twitter account!

Creating a new Facebook post from the ESP8266

In the last project of this chapter, we are going to see how to interact with Facebook from the ESP8266 Wi-Fi chip, via Temboo. We will see how to simply post a status update, but you can use it to post something on a friend's wall, post data on a page, and much more!

1. The first step is to create a Facebook app. You can do so by going to:

    ```
    https://developers.facebook.com/
    ```

2. From there, click on **Add a New App**:

3. When the interface asks you for the type of app, choose **Website**:

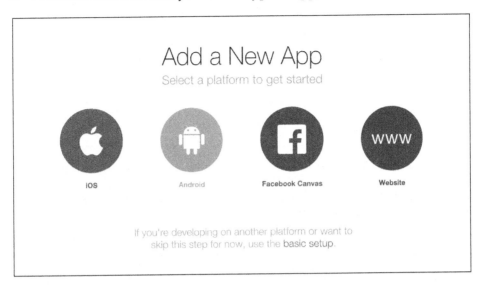

4. Then, give your app a name:

5. You will then be asked for a URL. This doesn't matter (it won't be used by the project), and you can put whatever you wish:

6. After that step, your app will be created. What you need to get here is the app ID and app secret, which should appear inside the application dashboard:

7. Then, go to **Setting**, and find **Client OAuth Settings**. Add the URL given in this screenshot as a callback URL, by replacing the Temboo username:

8. You're all set on the Facebook side! Now, go back to Temboo:

   `https://www.temboo.com/library/Library/Facebook/OAuth/`

9. This page will simply allow you to get a Facebook access token. First, enter the app ID (which you got earlier from the Facebook website) and scope (use `publish_actions`):

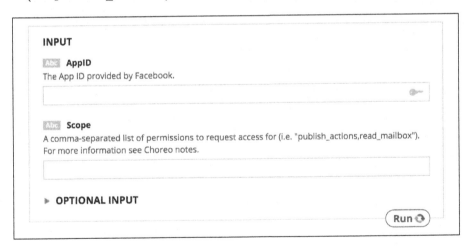

10. After that, you will be asked to follow a link. Do so, authorize the app, and then go back to the final authorization page and enter all the required data:

11. After clicking on **Run**, you will finally get your access token:

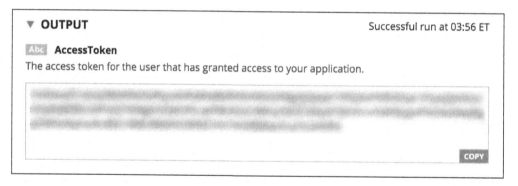

12. Now, go to the `Temboo` library that we actually want to use, which is the library to publish a post on Facebook:

    `https://temboo.com/library/Library/Facebook/Publishing/Post/`

13. From there, enter your access token, and also a message that you want the ESP8266 to post on your wall:

This is how it should look at the end:

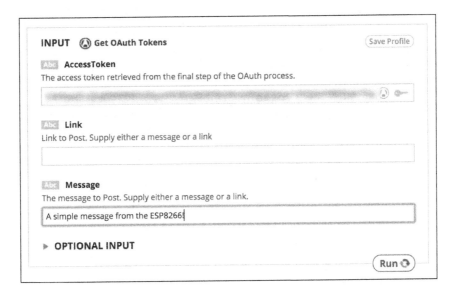

14. You can then generate the code and download it. Just as earlier, there are only two things we'll need to modify inside the code. The only thing you need to modify here is the Wi-Fi library:

```
#include <SPI.h>
#include <ESP8266WiFi.h>
#include <Temboo.h>
#include "TembooAccount.h" // Contains Temboo account information
```

15. Then, inside the `loop()` function, we post the message on the Facebook wall at every iteration of the loop:

```
if (numRuns <= maxRuns) {
    Serial.println("Running Post - Run #" + String(numRuns++));

    TembooChoreo PostChoreo(client);

    // Invoke the Temboo client
    PostChoreo.begin();

    // Set Temboo account credentials
    PostChoreo.setAccountName(TEMBOO_ACCOUNT);
    PostChoreo.setAppKeyName(TEMBOO_APP_KEY_NAME);
    PostChoreo.setAppKey(TEMBOO_APP_KEY);

    // Set Choreo inputs
    String MessageValue = "A simple message from the ESP8266!";
    PostChoreo.addInput("Message", MessageValue);
    String AccessTokenValue = "accessToken";
    PostChoreo.addInput("AccessToken", AccessTokenValue);

    // Identify the Choreo to run
    PostChoreo.setChoreo("/Library/Facebook/Publishing/Post");

    // Run the Choreo; when results are available, print them to
    serial
    PostChoreo.run();

    while(PostChoreo.available()) {
      char c = PostChoreo.read();
      Serial.print(c);
    }
    PostChoreo.close();
}
```

```
Serial.println("\nWaiting...\n");
delay(30000); // wait 30 seconds between Post calls
}
```

16. It's now time to finally test this project! Upload the code to the board, and then check your Facebook profile. After a while, you should see a new post appearing on your wall, with the message we defined in the sketch:

You can now use Temboo to post on Facebook using the ESP8266 Wi-Fi chip!

Summary

In this chapter, we learned how to interact with web services from the ESP8266 chip. We learned how to post data on Twitter, how to grab weather data from Yahoo, and also how to interact with Facebook.

I really recommend you now play with all the libraries that are offered by Temboo. The possibilities are nearly endless. You can, for example, have a Faceboook page that's just for your home, and that you use to automatically post data about your home! You can also simply use the extra data provided by those services (for example weather data) to enrich your own projects.

In the next chapter, we are going to learn about another important part of the Internet of Things: machine-to-machine communications.

6
Machine-to-Machine Communications

In the previous chapters, we learned how to make the ESP8266 log data online, and also how to control it remotely from anywhere in the world. However, all those Internet of Things projects had something in common: they required your intervention at some point, either to look at the data or to click on buttons to control the device remotely.

In this chapter, we are going to look at another field of the Internet of Things: **Machine-to-Machine (M2M)** communications. Those are the cases where no human intervention is required, and when machines communicate directly with each other to accomplish particular tasks.

And this is exactly what we are going to illustrate with ESP8266 boards in this chapter. We are first going to make a very simple project to illustrate M2M communications, and then we are going to apply this knowledge to build a light-activated relay, based on two ESP8266 boards. Let's start!

Hardware and software requirements

For this project, you will of course need an ESP8266 chip. As for most of this book, I used the Adafruit Huzzah ESP8266 module, but any ESP8266 module will work fine here.

For the first project of this chapter, you will need an LED, along with a 330 Ohm resistor. You will also need a mini push button and a 1K Ohm resistor.

For the second project of this chapter, you will need a relay, a 10K Ohm resistor, and a small photocell.

You will also need a 3.3V/5V FTDI USB module to program the ESP8266 chip.

Finally, you will also need some jumper wires and a breadboard.

This is a list of all the components that will be used in this chapter:

- Adafruit ES8266 module (x2) (`https://www.adafruit.com/products/2471`)
- FTDI USB module (`https://www.adafruit.com/products/284`)
- LED (`https://www.sparkfun.com/products/9590`)
- 330 Ohm resistor (`https://www.sparkfun.com/products/8377`)
- Relay (`https://www.sparkfun.com/products/10747`)
- Photocell (`https://www.sparkfun.com/products/9088`)
- 10K Ohm resistor (`https://www.sparkfun.com/products/8374`)
- Mini push button (`https://www.sparkfun.com/products/97`)
- 1K Ohm resistor (`https://www.sparkfun.com/products/8980`)
- Breadboard (x2) (`https://www.sparkfun.com/products/12002`)
- Jumper wires (`https://www.sparkfun.com/products/9194`)

On the software side, if it's not been done yet, you will need to install the latest version of the Arduino IDE, which you can get from:

`http://www.arduino.cc/en/Main/Software`

Then, you will also need to have the aREST and `PubSubClient` libraries installed. To install a library, simply use the Arduino library manager.

To make the ESP8266 chips talk to each other, we are also going to use the IFTTT web service. IFTTT is a service where you can create recipes that will perform a given action when a given trigger is received, which is perfect for M2M communications. If it's not been done yet, create an account at IFTTT:

`https://ifttt.com/`

Over there, you can already add the **Maker** channel to your account. This will make sure that it is available for your recipes, and you will also receive a key that you will need to use later in the chapter.

Simple machine-to-machine communication

In the first project of this chapter, we are going to see a very simple case of M2M communication, where one ESP8266 Wi-Fi chip will send a trigger signal to another chip (via the cloud, of course), that will in response toggle the state of an LED. For the trigger, we'll use a simple push button connected to the first ESP8266.

Let's first assemble the hardware for this project. For the LED board, the hardware configuration is really easy: simply place the resistor in series with the LED, just as we already did in earlier chapters. Then, connect the resistor to pin 5 of the ESP8266, and the other pin to the ground.

This is the final result for the LED board:

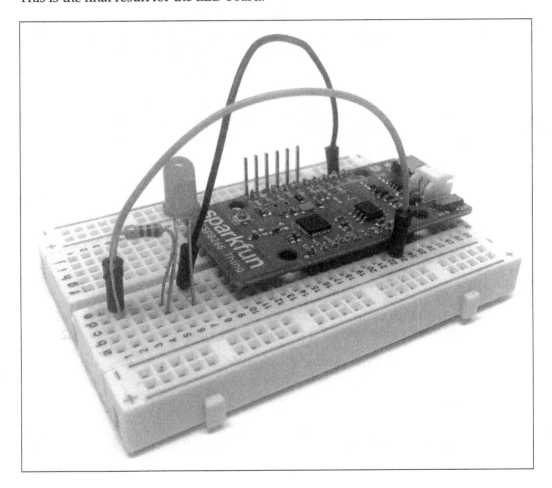

For the board that will host the push button, first place the push button on the board, as well as the ESP8266. Then, connect the resistor to one side of the push button, and the other side of the resistor to the ground. Also connect pin 5 of this ESP8266 Wi-Fi chip to this side of the push button. Finally, connect the other side of the push button to the VCC pin of the ESP8266.

This is the final result for the board with the push button:

We are now going to configure both boards so they can communicate with each other. As I said earlier, we are going to use the IFTTT service to make the two boards talk to each other.

We are first going to configure the LED board so it can receive commands from the cloud. For that, we'll use the aREST framework once again:

1. This sketch starts by importing the required libraries:

    ```
    #include <ESP8266WiFi.h>
    #include <PubSubClient.h>
    #include <aREST.h>
    ```

2. Next, we create the required clients to connect to the cloud:

    ```
    WiFiClient espClient;
    PubSubClient client(espClient);
    ```

3. We also initialize the aREST library:

```
aREST rest = aREST(client);
```

4. Next, we give a unique ID to the device:

```
char* device_id = "01e47f";
```

You also need to need to enter your Wi-Fi network credentials here:

```
const char* ssid = "wifi-name";
const char* password = "wifi-password";
```

5. Next, we define a Boolean variable to hold the current state of the LED:

```
bool ledState;
```

We also define a function to toggle the LED, which we will implement later:

```
int toggle(String command);
```

6. In the `setup()` function of the sketch, we expose the toggle function to aREST, and also connect the chip to the Wi-Fi network:

```
void setup(void)
{

  // Start Serial
  Serial.begin(115200);

  // Set callback
  client.setCallback(callback);

  // Give name and ID to device
  rest.set_id(device_id);
  rest.set_name("led");

  // Function
  rest.function("toggle", toggle);

  // LED state
  ledState = false;

  // Connect to WiFi
  WiFi.begin(ssid, password);
  while (WiFi.status() != WL_CONNECTED) {
    delay(500);
    Serial.print(".");
  }
```

```
Serial.println("");
Serial.println("WiFi connected");

// Pin 5 as output
pinMode(5, OUTPUT);

}
```

7. In the `loop()` function of the sketch, we simply keep the connection with the aREST cloud platform:

```
void loop() {

  // Connect to the cloud
  rest.handle(client);

}
```

8. At the end, we also need to implement the function to toggle the LED. We simply invert the state of the LED when the function is called, and then we also apply this new state to the LED:

```
// Toggle LED
int toggle(String command) {

  ledState = !ledState;
  digitalWrite(5, ledState);
  return 1;
}
```

You can also grab this code from the GitHub repository of the book:

```
https://github.com/openhomeautomation/iot-esp8266-packt
```

Then, modify the credentials inside the code, and upload it to the board on which the LED is located.

Now, we are going to see how to configure the board on which the push button is located, which will trigger an event at IFTTT whenever the button is pressed:

1. This starts by including the ESP8266 Wi-Fi library:

```
#include <ESP8266WiFi.h>
```

2. Next, you also need to define your Wi-Fi credentials:

```
const char* ssid = "wifi-name";
const char* password = "wifi-pass";
```

3. You also need to insert your IFTTT key at this point:

```
const char* host = "maker.ifttt.com";
const char* eventName = "button_pressed";
const char* key = "ifttt-key";
```

4. In the `setup()` function of the sketch, we simply connect the ESP8266 to your Wi-Fi network:

```
void setup() {
  Serial.begin(115200);
  delay(10);

  // We start by connecting to a WiFi network

  Serial.println();
  Serial.println();
  Serial.print("Connecting to ");
  Serial.println(ssid);

  WiFi.begin(ssid, password);

  while (WiFi.status() != WL_CONNECTED) {
    delay(500);
    Serial.print(".");
  }

  Serial.println("");
  Serial.println("WiFi connected");
  Serial.println("IP address: ");
  Serial.println(WiFi.localIP());

  // Pin 5 as input
  pinMode(5, INPUT);
}
```

5. In the `loop()` function of the sketch, we check whether the button has been pressed:

```
if (digitalRead(5)) {
```

6. If that's the case, we send a message to IFTTT. We first connect to their servers and create a request:

```
// Use WiFiClient class to create TCP connections
WiFiClient client;
const int httpPort = 80;
if (!client.connect(host, httpPort)) {
```

```
    Serial.println("connection failed");
    return;
}


// We now create a URI for the request
String url = "/trigger/";
url += eventName;
url += "/with/key/";
url += key;

Serial.print("Requesting URL: ");
Serial.println(url);
```

7. Once that's done, we actually send the request to IFTTT:

```
client.print(String("GET ") + url + " HTTP/1.1\r\n" +
            "Host: " + host + "\r\n" +
            "Connection: close\r\n\r\n");
int timeout = millis() + 5000;
while (client.available() == 0) {
  if (timeout - millis() < 0) {
    Serial.println(">>> Client Timeout !");
    client.stop();
    return;
  }
}
```

8. To end the request, we read the data coming back from IFTTT and print it:

```
while(client.available()){
  String line = client.readStringUntil('\r');
  Serial.print(line);
}

Serial.println();
Serial.println("closing connection");
}
```

9. You can now also grab the sketch from the GitHub repository for the book and upload it to the board.

   However, for now, our two boards are not communicating with each other. This is why we are now going to go to IFTTT in order to create a recipe to link those two boards.

10. On the IFTTT website, create a new recipe and choose the **Maker** channel as the trigger:

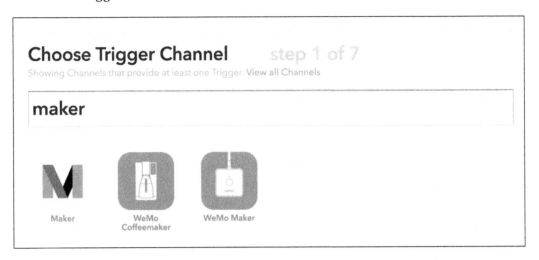

11. Next, choose **Receive a web request** as the trigger type:

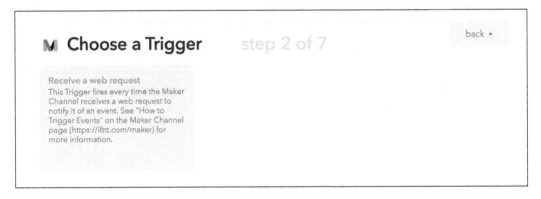

12. As the event, enter `button_pressed`, which is also what we entered inside the Arduino sketch:

13. As the action channel, also choose the **Maker** channel:

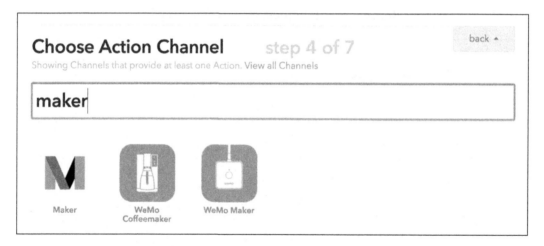

14. For the action, select **Make a web request**:

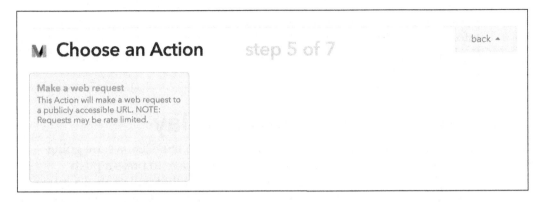

15. For the action parameters, we basically need to call the function on the device we created. Therefore, simply enter the parameters just as seen in this screenshot:

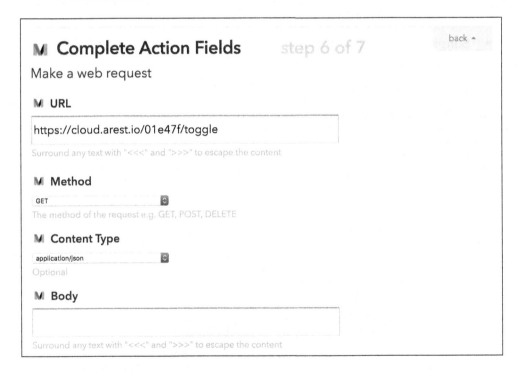

16. You of course need to modify the URL with the device ID you set inside the code. After that, create the recipe, which should now appear inside your IFTTT account.

17. You can now finally test the project, as IFTTT is now making the link between our two boards. Just press on the push button, and should quickly see that the LED will come on. Note that this can take 2-3 seconds, as the information needs to go through the IFTTT servers first. You can also press the button again to switch the LED off. You have now built your first basic M2M communication project!

Building a light-activated relay

Now that we know how to build M2M projects using the ESP8266, we are going to apply it to a simple project, in which you won't even have to press a push button at all. We are going to build a light-activated relay that will control a relay connected to one ESP8266 module depending on the light level measured by another ESP8266. This project will simulate a part of a home automation system, where you automatically want to switch the lights on when it's getting dark outside.

First, we need to assemble both boards. Let's start with the board that will host the relay, as it is the easiest one to assemble:

- Simply connect the VCC pin of the relay to the VCC pin of the ESP8266
- GND to GND
- SIG or EN pin of the relay to pin 5 of the ESP8266

This is the result for this board:

For the board that will host the photocell, first place the ESP8266 on the breadboard, and then the 10K Ohm resistor in series with the photocell on the breadboard as well. Then, connect the common pin of the photocell and the resistor to pin *A* or *ADC* of the ESP8266, which is the analog input pin on the ESP8266 board. Then, connect the other end of the photocell to VCC, and the other end of the resistor to GND.

This is the final result for this board:

Let's now see how to configure those boards. For the relay board, you can simply use the same sketch as for the LED board in the previous project, as we are again going to use the aREST cloud server.

For the photocell board, it will be very similar to the push button board in the first project, so we will only talk about the main differences here.

First, we set a variable that will define whether the light level is currently *low* or *high*. We'll set it to *low* by default, by assigning a `false` value to the variable:

```
bool lightLevel = false;
```

In the `loop()` function of the sketch, we first measure the state of the analog pin, and we print it on the Serial monitor:

```
Serial.print("Light level: ");
Serial.println(analogRead(A0));
```

Next, we check whether the light level is below a given threshold, and also whether the previous light level state was *high*. Note that the threshold is arbitrary here, it is just to illustrate M2M communications between the two boards. If we are indeed in those conditions, we send an event, `light_level_low`:

```
if (analogRead(A0) < 700 && lightLevel) {

    lightLevel = false;
    makeRequest("light_level_low");

}
```

On the other end, if the light level is *high*, and we were in the *low* state before, we send a `light_level_high` event to IFTTT:

```
if (analogRead(A0) > 800 && !lightLevel) {

    lightLevel = true;
    makeRequest("light_level_high");

}
```

You can now configure the board with the photocell using this code, which you can also find in the GitHub repository for the book. Again, we now need to create recipes on IFTTT to link the two boards.

Go to IFTTT again and create a new recipe. Again, use the **Maker** channel as the trigger, and set the event name to `light_level_low` as defined in the sketch:

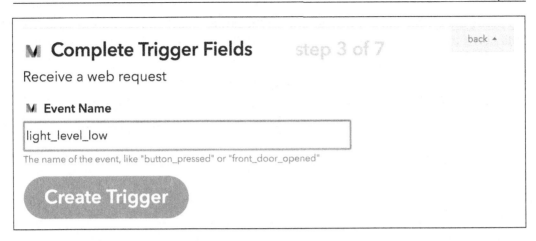

For the action, select the **Maker** channel again, and create a web request with the following parameters:

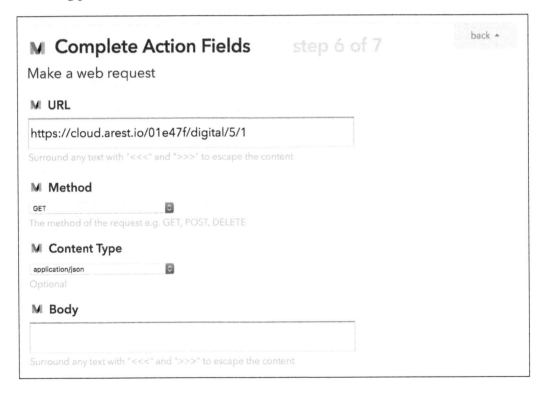

Here, we are setting pin 5 to a *high* state on the target board, as we want to switch the relay on if the light levels are *low*. Of course, make sure to change the device ID of your device inside the URL to be called by IFTTT.

Create the recipe, and do exactly the same with the other scenario by creating another recipe. This time, choose `light_level_high` as the trigger event:

For the action, enter exactly the same request as before, but this time with a *0* at the end, as we want to switch the lights off if the light level gets *high* again:

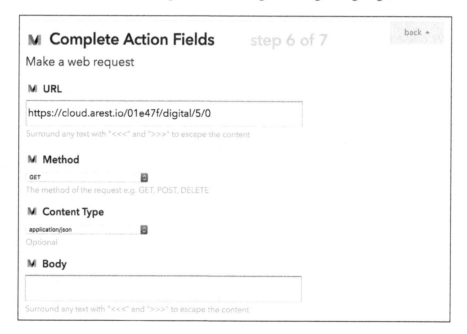

You should now see both recipes active inside your IFTTT dashboard:

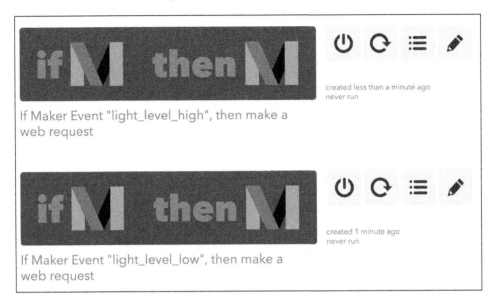

You can now test the project! To simulate it being *dark* outside, just place your hand on top of the photocell. You should see that 2-3 seconds after that, the relay should automatically switch to an active state on the other board. If you remove your hand, the relay should switch off again. Note that because we are using M2M communications via a cloud service, both boards can of course be placed in different locations. For example, you could easily have one board outside and one inside your home, even if that means they are connected to different Wi-Fi networks.

Summary

Let's summarize what we achieved in this project. We saw how to implement M2M communications using the ESP8266 Wi-Fi chip. We illustrated this by building two simple projects that used IFTTT to make the link between the ESP8266 boards.

You can of course now use what you learned inside this project to build your own Machine-to-Machine projects. M2M communications is a very wide topic, and there are so many things you can implement with it. For example, you could build a complete security system based in the cloud, with just ESP8266 modules communicating with each other, each equipped with a motion sensor. This is something we are also going to see later in the book.

In the next chapter, we are going to again use IFTTT, but for another purpose: sending automated notifications from your ESP8266 projects.

7
Sending Notifications from the ESP8266

In this chapter, we are going to see how to integrate a very important element of the IoT with the ESP8266: notifications. IoT devices constantly alert users when something significant is happening, or simply at regular intervals, for example to report data.

We are going to see three scenarios in this chapter. First, we'll see how to send simple e-mail notifications from the ESP8266. Then, we'll learn how to make the chip regularly send data via text messages to your phone. Finally, we will see how to send alerts via push notifications. Let's start!

Hardware and software requirements

For this project, you will of course need an ESP8266 chip. As for most of this book, I used the Adafruit Huzzah ESP8266 module, but any ESP8266 module will work fine here.

As a sensor, I'll use the DHT11 sensor here just to illustrate the behavior of two out of the three scenarios in this chapter. However, you could use any sensor, or even use dummy data for this chapter. The goal is really to learn how to send notifications.

You will also need a 3.3V/5V FTDI USB module to program the ESP8266 chip.

Finally, you will also need some jumper wires and a breadboard.

This is a list of all the components that will be used in this chapter:

- Adafruit ES8266 module (`https://www.adafruit.com/products/2471`)
- FTDI USB module (`https://www.adafruit.com/products/284`)
- DHT11 sensor (`https://www.adafruit.com/products/386`)
- Breadboard (`https://www.sparkfun.com/products/12002`)
- Jumper wires (`https://www.sparkfun.com/products/9194`)

On the software side, if it's not been done yet, you will need to install the latest version of the Arduino IDE, which you can get from here:

`http://www.arduino.cc/en/Main/Software`

Then, you will need to have an IFTTT account, which we will use for all the projects in this chapter. IFTTT is a very cool web service that can put two web services in contact via "recipes" that are activated by a trigger (the `If`) which in return triggers an action (the that).

To create an account, simply go to:

`https://ifttt.com/recipes`

You will then be able to create your free account:

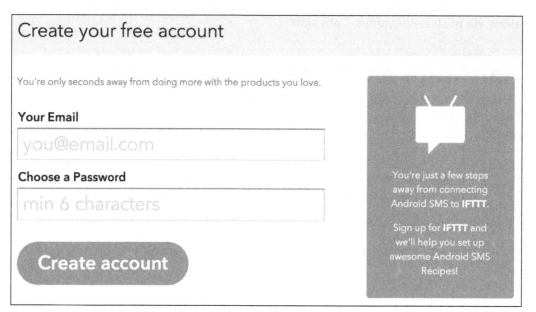

Hardware configuration

Let's now configure the hardware for this project. As this is something we already saw in earlier chapters, I will refer you to *Chapter 5, Interacting With Web Services,* to learn how to assemble the hardware for this project.

This is how it should look at the end:

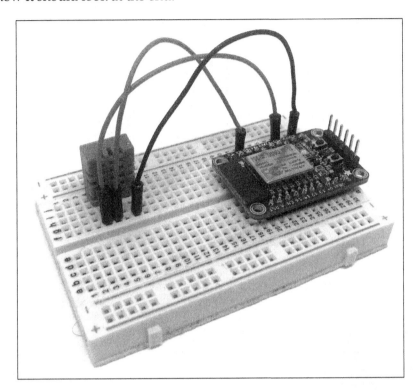

Sending an e-mail notification

It's now time to make our first project: sending e-mail notifications! For this first approach to notifications, we'll simply send a message at regular intervals to the e-mail address of your choice.

To connect the ESP8266 to IFTTT, we need a channel called **Maker**, which is available on IFTTT. You first need to go to the **Channels** tab and find this channel:

Once the channel is opened on your screen, you need to connect it to your IFTTT account:

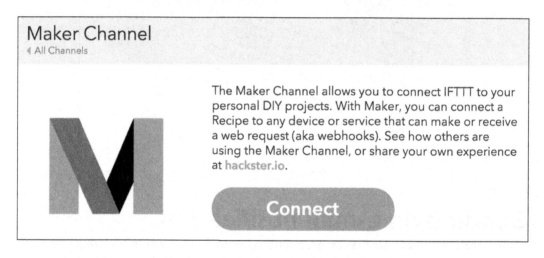

This will allow you to get a key for your **Maker Channel**:

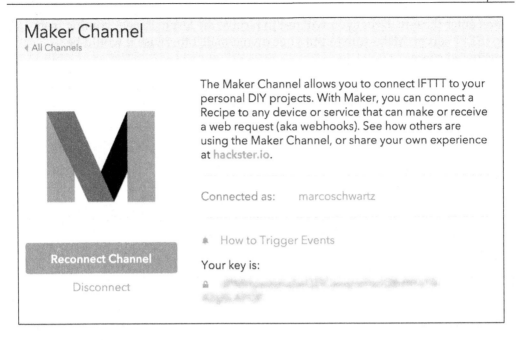

Make sure you have this key to hand; you'll need it really soon. As for all channels, you only need to do this once.

The next channel we'll add is the **Email Channel**:

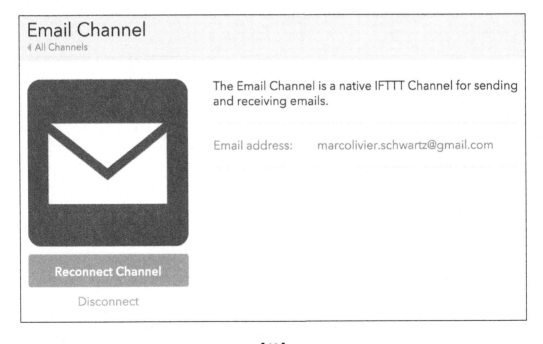

Here, enter the e-mail that you will use to receive the test messages coming from the IFTTT server. Make sure to put your own e-mail, otherwise it would be considered spam.

Then, we can create a **recipe** that will link the **Maker Channel** to sending an e-mail. Simply click on the following button on the main page:

From the screen where you can create a new recipe, select the **Maker** channel we connected earlier:

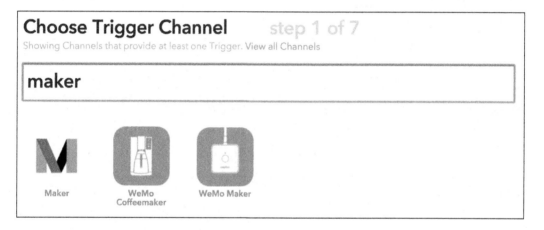

As a trigger, we'll simply write `hello`:

For the **Action Channel**, select the e-mail channel you added earlier:

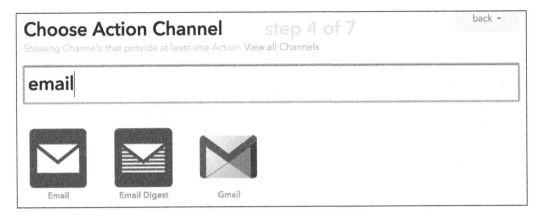

Then, you will be asked to fill in the action channel with what e-mail you want to send. As we just want to test notifications here, simply enter a simple message:

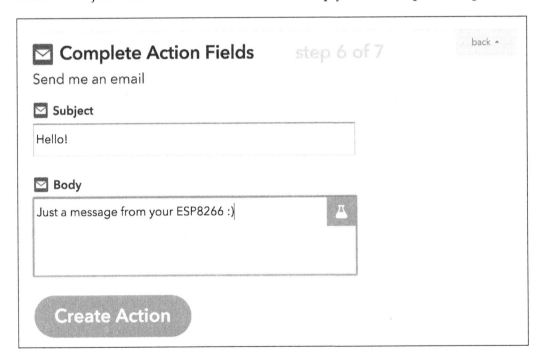

You can now save the recipe, which will appear inside your IFTTT dashboard:

Now that the recipe is active, it's time to build the Arduino sketch to actually activate this recipe. As usual, I'll detail the most important parts of the sketch here:

1. It starts by including the ESP8266 Wi-Fi library:

```
#include <ESP8266WiFi.h>
```

2. Then, you need to insert your Wi-Fi `name` and `password`:

```
const char* ssid     = "wifi-name";
const char* password = "wifi-pass";
```

3. After that, you need to put in some information about IFTTT, such as the event name and your IFTTT **Maker** channel key:

```
const char* host = "maker.ifttt.com";
const char* eventName  = "hello";
const char* key = "your-key";
```

4. Now, in the `setup()` function, we connect the ESP8266 to the Wi-Fi network:

```
Serial.println();
  Serial.println();
  Serial.print("Connecting to ");
  Serial.println(ssid);
```

```
WiFi.begin(ssid, password);

while (WiFi.status() != WL_CONNECTED) {
  delay(500);
  Serial.print(".");
}

Serial.println("");
Serial.println("WiFi connected");
Serial.println("IP address: ");
Serial.println(WiFi.localIP());
```

5. In the `loop()` function, we first connect to the IFTTT server:

```
WiFiClient client;
const int httpPort = 80;
if (!client.connect(host, httpPort)) {
  Serial.println("connection failed");
  return;
}
```

6. Then, we prepare the request with the event name:

```
String url = "/trigger/";
url += eventName;
url += "/with/key/";
url += key;
```

7. We can then send the request to the server:

```
client.print(String("GET ") + url + " HTTP/1.1\r\n" +
             "Host: " + host + "\r\n" +
             "Connection: close\r\n\r\n");
int timeout = millis() + 5000;
while (client.available() == 0) {
  if (timeout - millis() < 0) {
    Serial.println(">>> Client Timeout !");
    client.stop();
    return;
  }
}
```

8. And we read the answer from the server:

```
while(client.available()){
    String line = client.readStringUntil('\r');
    Serial.print(line);
}

Serial.println();
Serial.println("closing connection");
```

9. Finally, we wait one minute before each send:

```
delay(60 * 1000);
```

It's now finally time to test the project! Grab the code from the GitHub repository for the book:

```
https://github.com/openhomeautomation/iot-esp8266-packt
```

Then, modify the code with your own Wi-Fi settings and IFTTT data. Upload the code to the board. Open the serial monitor, and you should see that the board is connected to the IFTTT servers and receiving the confirmation that the event has been triggered:

Now, check your e-mail inbox. You should see that you just received a message from your ESP8266:

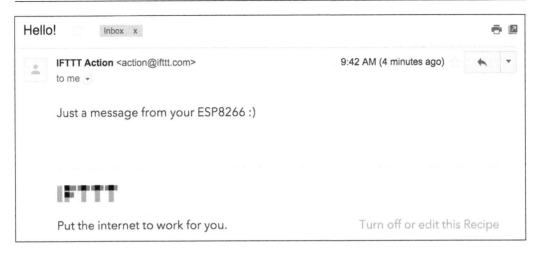

Of course, make sure to quickly disconnect your ESP8266 or shut down the recipe, or you will be spammed by your own project!

Sending data via text message

We are now going to use the same hardware to make a completely different project. We'll use IFTTT again to send measurement data from the ESP8266 chip to your mobile phone:

1. To do that, the first step is to connect the SMS channel to your IFTTT account. It's very simple, and you will just have to put in your phone number:

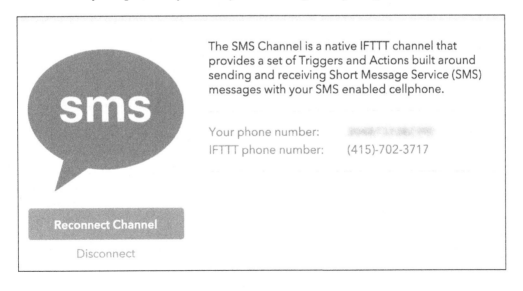

2. It's now time to create a new recipe. This time, use **data** as the name of the event:

3. Then, select the newly created **SMS** channel as the action of the recipe:

4. Now, we are going to build a more complex message than earlier, because we want to have the information about the measurements done by the ESP8266 in the message. Thanks to IFTTT, it's very easy using the assistant to add values coming from the trigger channel:

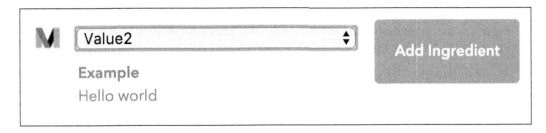

5. This is how your message should look at the end:

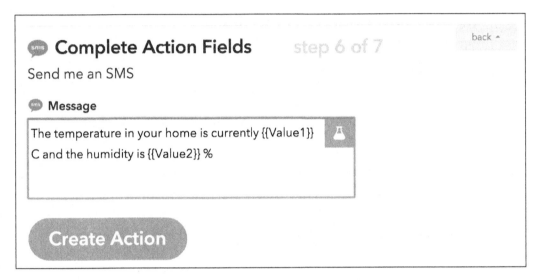

6. Finally, create the recipe:

Now that the recipe is active, we can move on to the creation of the Arduino sketch. As there are many elements in common with the previous sketch, I will only detail the important elements here:

1. You need to include the DHT library:

    ```
    #include "DHT.h"
    ```

2. Then, we set the DHT sensor pin and type:

    ```
    #define DHTPIN 5
    #define DHTTYPE DHT11
    ```

3. We also create an instance of the DHT sensor:

    ```
    DHT dht(DHTPIN, DHTTYPE, 15);
    ```

4. This time, we name the event `data`:

    ```
    const char* eventName    = "data";
    ```

5. In the `setup()` function of the sketch, we initialize the DHT sensor:

    ```
    dht.begin();
    ```

6. Then, inside the `loop()` function, we measure data from the sensor:

    ```
    float h = dht.readHumidity();
    float t = dht.readTemperature();
    ```

7. After that, we put the data that was just measured into the request:

    ```
    String url = "/trigger/";
      url += eventName;
      url += "/with/key/";
      url += key;
      url += "?value1=";
      url += String(t);
      url += "&value2=";
      url += String(h);
    ```

It's now time to test the sketch! Grab it from the GitHub repository for the book, and make sure to modify the sketch with your Wi-Fi settings and IFTTT data.

Then, upload the code to the board. After a few moments, you should receive a message on your mobile phone showing the data that was measured:

> Today 10:07
>
> The temperature in your home is currently 31.00 C and the humidity is 34.00 %

Receiving alerts via push notifications

In the last project of the chapter, we are going to see how to send a third type of notification: push notifications. These are perfect for important alerts, as they will show up right on your phone when they're triggered.

To do so, we'll be using an application called Pushover that exists for iOS and Android. You first need to create an account at:

```
https://pushover.net/
```

Inside the Pushover dashboard, you'll need to get the API key; you'll need it in a moment to link Pushover to your IFTTT account.

Inside IFTTT, you can now connect the **Pushover** channel:

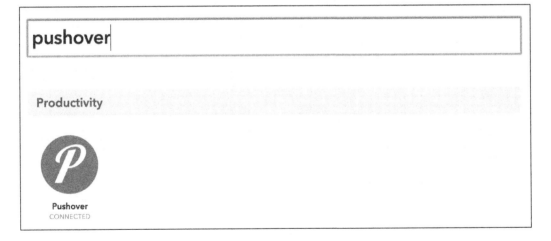

Now, we are ready to create the final recipe for this chapter. As the event name, this time choose **alert**:

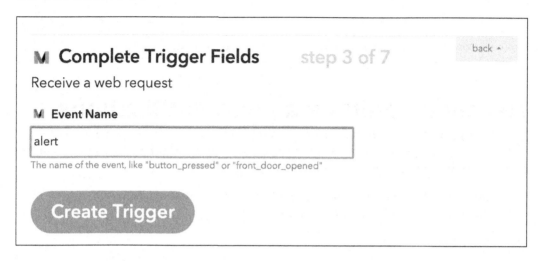

Then, as the action channel, select the **Pushover** channel:

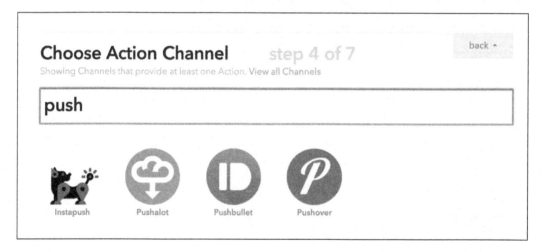

As the message for the push notification, you can choose what you want, for example a message saying that the humidity is too high:

Finally, save the recipe, which should now appear on your dashboard:

Let's now configure the ESP8266 board. As the sketch is really similar to the sketches we already saw, I will only tell you about what changed here.

The first thing we need to change is the name of the event sent to IFTTT:

```
const char* eventName    = "alert";
```

Then, we set up the board to send an alert whenever the humidity rises above 30%:

```
if (h > 30.00) {
```

We also need to add a bigger delay when the alert is triggered, just to make sure you don't receive an alert every 5 seconds:

```
delay(10 * 60 * 1000);
```

It's finally time to test the project! Grab the code from GitHub, and change the Wi-Fi settings and also the IFTTT data. Then, upload the code to the board.

If the humidity is indeed above the threshold, you should receive a notification pretty soon on your phone:

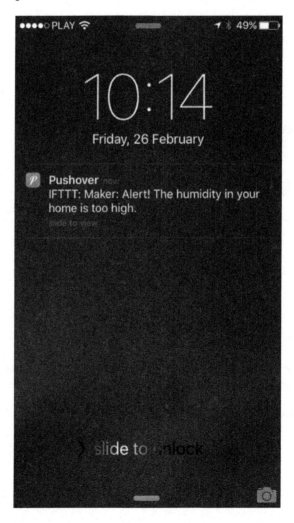

This is much better than just an e-mail, as you'll see it even if you are not currently checking e-mails or text messages. Therefore, it's just perfect for urgent alerts, and you now know how to send those alerts right from your ESP8266.

Summary

In this chapter, we saw how to send automated notifications from your ESP8266 to your e-mail, your phone via text messages, and via push notifications. This allows us to either send data back to our mobile devices or create alerts based on measured data.

You can of course adapt what you learned in this project to your needs, and create alerts coming from your ESP8266 (or from several modules!) that will let you know instantly about any changes in what you want to monitor.

In the next chapter, we are going to take everything we've learned so far and create a new project using the ESP8266: a door lock that you can control from the cloud.

8
Controlling a Door Lock from the Cloud

This will be the first project of this book in which we'll take everything we learned so far and integrate it to make a complete Internet of Things project you can actually use in your life.

For this project, we are going to build a door lock that we can control from anywhere on the planet using the ESP8266 Wi-Fi chip. We are also going to see how to integrate notifications right into the software you'll build, so you will receive a push notification in case anyone opens the door lock. Let's start!

Hardware and software requirements

For this project, you will of course need an ESP8266 chip. As for most of this book, I used the Adafruit Huzzah ESP8266 module, but any ESP8266 module will work fine here.

For the lock, I used a 12V DC solenoid-based door lock. You can, of course, use any other equivalent lock on the market. You will need a few components to use the lock: an NPN transistor, a protection diode, and a 1K Ohm resistor. I included the reference for all those components in this section. You will also need a 12V DC power supply that you can connect to a breadboard.

This is a picture of the lock that I will be using for this project:

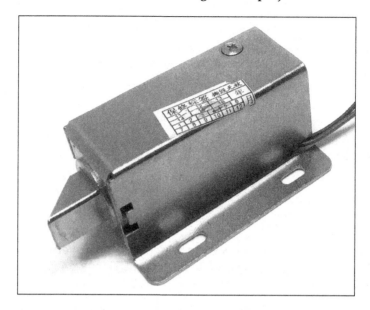

You will also need a 3.3V/5V FTDI USB module to program the ESP8266 chip.

Finally, you will also need some jumper wires and a breadboard.

This is a list of all the components that will be used in this chapter:

- Adafruit ES8266 module (`https://www.adafruit.com/products/2471`)
- FTDI USB module (`https://www.adafruit.com/products/284`)
- Lock Style Solenoid (`https://www.adafruit.com/products/1512`)
- NPN transistor (`https://www.sparkfun.com/products/13689`)
- Resistor (`https://www.sparkfun.com/products/8980`)
- Diode (`https://www.sparkfun.com/products/8589`)
- Breadboard (`https://www.sparkfun.com/products/12002`)
- Jumper wires (`https://www.sparkfun.com/products/9194`)

For the software, if it's not been done yet, you will need to install the latest version of the Arduino IDE, which you can get from here:

`http://www.arduino.cc/en/Main/Software`

Then, for the last part of the chapter, you will also need an IFTTT account. If you don't have one, please refer to the *Chapter 5, Interacting With Web Services* to learn how to create your IFTTT account.

Configuring the hardware

Let's now configure the hardware for this project. The configuration for this project is quite complex, which was why I included a schematic to help you out:

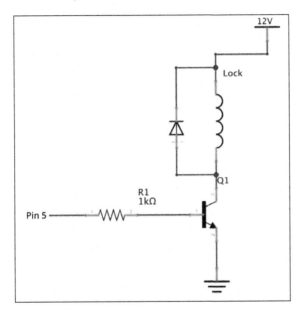

This schematic represents how you should connect the lock to the ESP8266. First, place the transistor on the breadboard, and connect the base of the transistor to the ESP8266 via the 1K Ohm resistor. Then, connect the emitter of the transistor to the ground of the ESP8266. After that, connect the door lock to the 12V DC power supply and to the remaining pin of the transistor. Finally, connect the diode in parallel to the lock, as indicated on the schematics. Note that on the diode, the cathode is usually marked with a grey stripe, corresponding to the schematics.

This is how it should look at the end:

Configuring the ESP8266 board

It's now time to configure the ESP8266 Wi-Fi chip so it can accept commands coming from the cloud. This is something we already saw earlier, but it's always good to remember the basics, as we'll make a more complicated sketch later in this chapter:

1. We first need to include the required libraries:

```
#include <ESP8266WiFi.h>
#include <PubSubClient.h>
#include <aREST.h>
```

2. Then, we declare a Wi-Fi client and PubSub (MQTT) client:

```
WiFiClient espClient;
PubSubClient client(espClient);
```

3. After that, we create an instance of the aREST library:

```
aREST rest = aREST(client);
```

4. You also need to enter your Wi-Fi name and password into the sketch:

```
const char* ssid = "wifi-ssid";
const char* password = "wifi-pass";
```

5. You can also give a name to your device:

```
rest.set_id(device_id);
rest.set_name("door_lock");
```

6. Finally, in the `loop()` function of the sketch, we handle the connection coming from the cloud:

```
rest.handle(client);
```

It's now time to configure the board! Simply grab the code from the GitHub repository for the book, make sure to modify the Wi-Fi settings and password, upload the code to the board, and leave it there; we'll use a dashboard to actually control the lock.

Controlling the lock from the cloud

It's now time to see how to control our door lock from the cloud. Again, we'll use the dashboard feature of aREST to rapidly build a cloud dashboard for our project:

1. Simply go to:

```
http://dashboard.arest.io/
```

2. After creating an account, you'll be able to create your first dashboard:

3. Once it's been created, simply click on the **name** of the new dashboard:

4. From there, you'll be able to create a new element. As we simply want on/off buttons here, configure your dashboard with the following settings: name the element `Lock`, enter the device ID of the project, and select the correct digital pin (5). This is all indicated in this screenshot:

5. Of course, make sure to replace the device ID with the one from your own device. Once that's done, you should see your new control inside the dashboard:

You can now finally try the project; simply click on the **On** button and the lock should immediately be activated. You can now lock or unlock a door from anywhere in the world! Just make sure that you are not clicking on different buttons too quickly; unlike an LED, for example, the door lock takes some time (one or two seconds) to respond.

Receiving notifications when the lock is opened

Controlling the lock from the cloud is great, but you can only find out its current state by opening the dashboard on your computer or mobile phone. But what if you are on the road, and the lock is attached to a quite important door in your home? You would want to be alerted when the door is opened.

This is exactly what we are going to do now using IFTTT. We are going to set up the board so it sends notifications to your smartphone when the door lock is opened:

1. First, go to IFTTT, and add two channels if that's not been done yet: the **Maker** channel and the **Pushover** channel. Also install the Pushover app on your smartphone. To learn more about this, refer to the *Chapter 7, Sending Notifications from the ESP8266*.

2. Then, create a new recipe, and choose the **Maker** channel as the trigger:

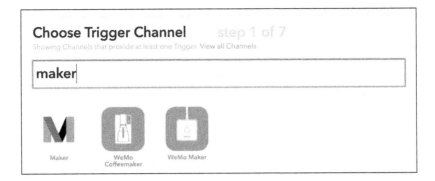

3. We need to use the **Maker** channel here, as it will allow us to use custom projects like ours with IFTTT. As the trigger for the channel, put the `lock_opened` event:

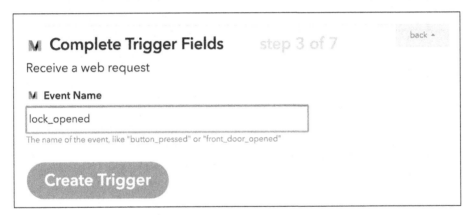

4. As the action, simply look for the **Pushover** channel, which we will again use to receive notifications from IFTTT:

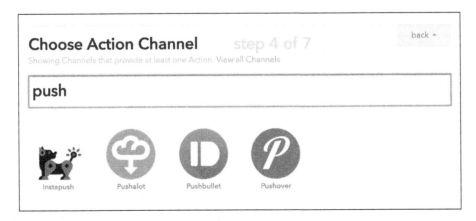

5. Then, select the notification type of your choice:

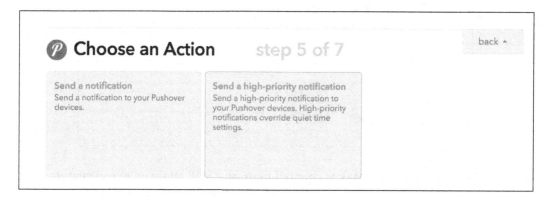

6. This will simply indicate to IFTTT whether it should send normal or high-priority notifications to your Pushover app. After that, put the message you want to receive every time an event is received:

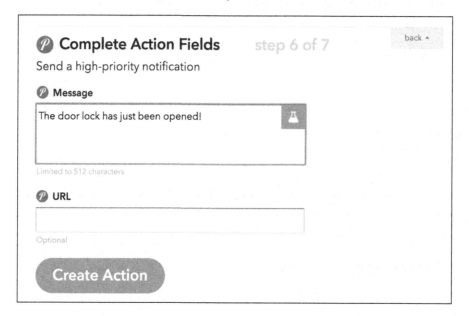

7. Finally, confirm the creation of the channel:

8. Let's now see what we need to add to the previous code to integrate the notifications. First, we need to define two variables to store the current status of the lock:

```
bool lockStatus;
bool previousLockStatus;
```

9. Then, inside the `setup()` function of the sketch, we read data from pin number 5, to check whether the lock is initially activated or not:

```
lockStatus = digitalRead(5);
previousLockStatus = lockStatus;
```

10. After that, inside the `loop()` function, we again read the state from pin number 5:

```
lockStatus = digitalRead(5);
```

11. If it has changed compared to the last read, and if the lock is open (which means that there is a LOW status on the pin), we send a notification via IFTTT:

```
if (lockStatus != previousLockStatus && lockStatus == 0) {

    Serial.print("connecting to ");
    Serial.println(host);
```

```
// Use WiFiClient class to create TCP connections
WiFiClient client;
const int httpPort = 80;
if (!client.connect(host, httpPort)) {
  Serial.println("connection failed");
  return;
}

// We now create a URI for the request
String url = "/trigger/";
url += eventName;
url += "/with/key/";
url += key;

Serial.print("Requesting URL: ");
Serial.println(url);

// This will send the request to the server
client.print(String("GET ") + url + " HTTP/1.1\r\n" +
             "Host: " + host + "\r\n" +
             "Connection: close\r\n\r\n");
int timeout = millis() + 5000;
while (client.available() == 0) {
  if (timeout - millis() < 0) {
    Serial.println(">>> Client Timeout !");
    client.stop();
    return;
  }
}

// Read all the lines of the reply from server and print them
to Serial
  while(client.available()){
    String line = client.readStringUntil('\r');
    Serial.print(line);
  }

  Serial.println();
  Serial.println("closing connection");

  // Set previous status
  previousLockStatus = lockStatus;

}
```

To learn more about how to send notifications via IFTTT, please check out *Chapter 7, Sending Notifications from the ESP8266.*

12. It's now time to test the project! Upload the code to the board, and then go back to the online dashboard that you used before to control the lock. This time, every time you open the lock, you should immediately get a notification on your smartphone.

This way, even if you shared your dashboard with somebody else, you will be informed when they open the door lock.

Summary

In this chapter, we saw how to use everything we learned so far in this book to build a project you can use in your home: a cloud-controlled door lock. We saw how to control the lock from anywhere in the world, and also how to make the project send notifications automatically to your smartphone when the lock is opened.

There are many ways to improve this project with what you learned in this chapter. One way is of course to add several locks to the same dashboard, and control them all from anywhere. You could also add a timer function to the project, and have the door open automatically between given time intervals (for example for a cleaner to come in).

In the next chapter, we'll see how to use your knowledge about the ESP8266 Wi-Fi chip to build another cool IoT project: a physical Bitcoin ticker.

9

Building a Physical Bitcoin Ticker

We already saw in this book that the ESP8266 Wi-Fi chip can be used in many different situations within the Internet of Things. In this chapter, we are going to use it for a quite exotic IoT project: getting the real-time price of Bitcoin, and displaying this price on a small OLED screen.

We are first going to see what Bitcoin is, and how we can grab the price of Bitcoin from a web service. Then, we'll configure our Bitcoin ticket and display the current price of Bitcoin on an OLED display. Finally, we'll add some LEDs into the project to check visually whether the price is going up or down. Let's start!

What is Bitcoin?

Before we actually start building the project itself, let's first quickly talk about Bitcoin, in case you don't know what it is yet.

Bitcoin is a virtual currency that emerged back in 2009. Unlike other virtual currencies that existed up to then, Bitcoin is protected by a global network of computers, all working with the same distributed ledger called the Blockchain, which guarantees every transaction made.

Since then, a lot of people and businesses around the world have started to accept Bitcoin as a way of payment. Bitcoin is also accepted in brick and mortar stores; for example, stores that display the **Bitcoin Accepted Here** sign:

Of course, Bitcoin is also traded on exchanges, and therefore has a price in USD, and in most of the main currencies. For example, at the time of writing this book, one Bitcoin was worth 417 US dollars.

Therefore, it could be quite interesting and fun to make a project to find out how much Bitcoin is currently worth, using the ESP8266 Wi-Fi chip. And that's exactly what we are going to do in this chapter.

Online Bitcoin services

Before starting with online Bitcoin services, we need to know how to actually get the current price (in US dollars) of Bitcoin.

On the Web, it's quite easy to get the price or the historical value of Bitcoin. For example, a good website to look at is Coindesk:

```
http://www.coindesk.com/price/
```

On this website, you have access to the current price of Bitcoin, and also nice graphs showing the historical value of Bitcoin:

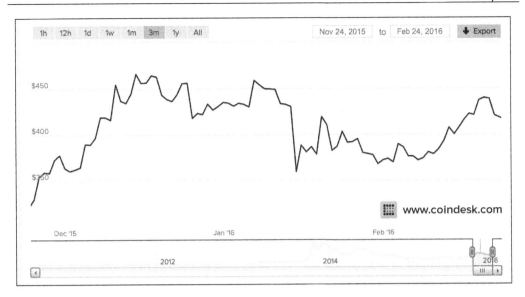

That's nice, but it is only accessible via the website and it's too complicated anyway for our little ESP8266 board.

A better solution is simply to have what is called a Bitcoin ticker that just displays the real-time value of Bitcoin. A good example of such a ticker can be found at the following URL:

```
http://preev.com/btc/usd
```

You will see the current value of Bitcoin, which you can display in multiple currencies:

1 BTC▾ = 417.4 USD▾

That's what we want to build for our project: a simple Bitcoin ticker that displays the current value of Bitcoin in USD.

However, we can't access this directly with the ESP8266. What we need is an **API (Application Programming Interface)**, which will return the current price of Bitcoin in a way that can be processed by our chip.

The best API I know to get this price is also from Coindesk, and can be accessed at:

`http://api.coindesk.com/v1/bpi/currentprice.json`

You can actually try it from a web browser. You will get a similar answer to this:

```
{
    "time":{
        "updated":"Feb 24, 2016 08:15:00 UTC",
        "updatedISO":"2016-02-24T08:15:00+00:00",
        "updateduk":"Feb 24, 2016 at 08:15 GMT"
    },
    "disclaimer":"This data was produced from the CoinDeskBitcoin Price
Index (USD). Non-USD currency data converted using hourly conversion
rate from openexchangerates.org",
    "bpi":{
        "USD":{
            "code":"USD",
            "symbol":"&#36;",
            "rate":"416.4970",
            "description":"United States Dollar",
            "rate_float":416.497
        },
        "GBP":{
            "code":"GBP",
            "symbol":"&pound;",
            "rate":"298.0036",
            "description":"British Pound Sterling",
            "rate_float":298.0036
        },
        "EUR":{
            "code":"EUR",
            "symbol":"&euro;",
            "rate":"378.1955",
            "description":"Euro",
            "rate_float":378.1955
        }
    }
}
```

You can see that this API returns the current price of Bitcoin, in several currencies. This is what we will use for our project to get the price of Bitcoin.

Hardware and software requirements

Let's now see the required components for this project. You will of course need an ESP8266 chip. As for most of this book, I used the Adafruit Huzzah ESP8266 module, but any ESP8266 module will work fine here.

You will also need an OLED display for the project. I used a 128x64 pixels monochrome OLED display, using the SSD1306 driver, which is the only one I know to be compatible with the ESP8266:

For the last part of the project, I used two LEDs, one red and one green, along with 330 Ohm resistors.

You will also need a 3.3V/5V FTDI USB module to program the ESP8266 chip.

Finally, you will also need some jumper wires and a breadboard.

This is a list of all the components that will be used in this project:

- Adafruit ES8266 module (`https://www.adafruit.com/products/2471`)
- FTDI USB module (`https://www.adafruit.com/products/284`)
- LED x 2 (`https://www.sparkfun.com/products/9590`)
- 330 Ohm resistor x 2 (`https://www.sparkfun.com/products/8377`)
- OLED display 128x64 pixels with the SSD1306 driver (`https://www.adafruit.com/products/326`)
- Breadboard (`https://www.sparkfun.com/products/12002`)
- Jumper wires (`https://www.sparkfun.com/products/9194`)

For the software, if it's not been done yet, you will need to install the latest version of the Arduino IDE.

Then, you will need a library to control the SSD1306 OLED screen. I recommend downloading it from the Arduino library manager, but you can also get it from the following repository:

`https://github.com/squix78/esp8266-oled-ssd1306`

Configuring the hardware

Let's now assemble the project:

1. First, place the ESP8266 module on the breadboard, along with the OLED screen.
2. Then, connect the power to the OLED screen: connect VIN to the 3.3V pin of the ESP8266, and GND to GND.
3. Next, we are going to connect the I2C pins the screen to the ESP8266. Connect the DATA pin of the screen to pin 14 of the ESP8266, and the CLK pin of the screen to pin 12 of the ESP8266.

 Note that some OLED screens can be configured to either use SPI or I2C. Make sure that your screen is configured to use I2C. This might require some soldering, depending on the brand of your display.

4. Finally, connect the RST pin of the OLED screen to pin 2 of the ESP8266 board. I found out that this is only necessary if you are having issues with the screen, but to be safe, connect this pin.

This is the final result:

Testing the ticker

We are now going to configure the project, and we'll start by going into the details of the code for this project. Of course, you will find all the code for this book inside the GitHub repository for the book.

It starts by including the required libraries:

```
#include <ESP8266WiFi.h>
#include <ArduinoJson.h>
#include <Wire.h>
#include "SSD1306.h"
```

Then, we define on which pin the OLED screen is connected:

```
#define SDA 14
#define SCL 12
#define I2C 0x3D
```

We also need to create an instance of the LCD display:

```
SSD1306 display(I2C, SDA, SCL);
```

To grab the current price of Bitcoin, we need to use the Coindesk API. Therefore, we have to define the URL of the API in the code:

```
const char* host = "api.coindesk.com";
```

You also need to modify the code to set your Wi-Fi name and password:

```
const char* ssid     = "wifi-network";
const char* password = "wif-password";
```

In the setup() function of the sketch, we initialize the

```
display.init();
display.flipScreenVertically();
display.clear();
display.display();
```

Still in the same function, we connect the board to your Wi-Fi network:

```
Serial.println();
Serial.println();
Serial.print("Connecting to ");
Serial.println(ssid);

WiFi.begin(ssid, password);

while (WiFi.status() != WL_CONNECTED) {
delay(500);
Serial.print(".");
  }

Serial.println("");
Serial.println("WiFi connected");
Serial.println("IP address: ");
Serial.println(WiFi.localIP());
```

In the loop() function of the sketch, we first connect to the API server:

```
WiFiClient client;
constinthttpPort = 80;
if (!client.connect(host, httpPort)) {
Serial.println("connection failed");
return;
  }
```

Then, we prepare the URL we'll actually call on the server. As we saw earlier in this chapter, we call the URL to get the current price:

```
String url = "/v1/bpi/currentprice.json";
```

After that, we actually send the request:

```
client.print(String("GET ") + url + " HTTP/1.1\r\n" +
             "Host: " + host + "\r\n" +
             "Connection: close\r\n\r\n");
```

Once the request is sent, we read whatever is coming back from the server:

```
String answer;
while(client.available()){
    String line = client.readStringUntil('\r');
answer += line;
   }

client.stop();
Serial.println();
Serial.println("closing connection");
```

Now that we have the answer from the server, it's time to process this answer. This starts by extracting the exact JSON answer from the raw answer:

```
String jsonAnswer;
intjsonIndex;

for (int i = 0; i <answer.length(); i++) {
if (answer[i] == '{') {
jsonIndex = i;
break;
    }
  }
```

Then, we extract the JSON object from the answer, and we store it in a string:

```
jsonAnswer = answer.substring(jsonIndex);
Serial.println();
Serial.println("JSON answer: ");
Serial.println(jsonAnswer);
jsonAnswer.trim();
```

From there, we can actually extract the Bitcoin price in USD, by doing some operations on the string containing the JSON object:

```
intrateIndex = jsonAnswer.indexOf("rate_float");
String priceString = jsonAnswer.substring(rateIndex + 12, rateIndex +
18);
priceString.trim();
float price = priceString.toFloat();
```

Finally, we display the price on the **Serial** monitor for debugging purposes:

```
Serial.println();
Serial.println("Bitcoin price: ");
Serial.println(price);
```

And we also display it on the screen, centered and in a large font:

```
display.clear();
display.setFont(ArialMT_Plain_24);
display.drawString(26, 20, priceString);
display.display();
```

We also want to avoid the sketch just repeating itself all the time. That's why you can adjust the delay between two updates:

```
delay(5000);
```

It's finally time to test the sketch! You can grab the whole code from the GitHub repository for the book:

```
https://github.com/openhomeautomation/iot-esp8266-packt
```

After making sure that you changed the Wi-Fi name and password inside the sketch, upload the code to the board.

Once that's done, open the **Serial** monitor. You should immediately see that the ESP8266 chip received the answer from the Coindesk server:

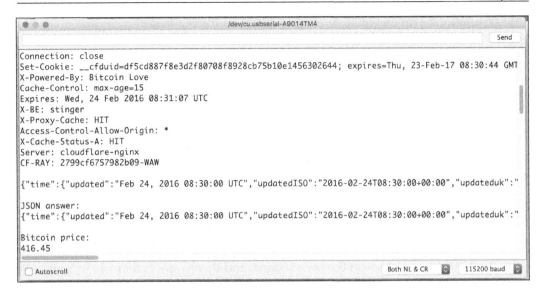

```
/dev/cu.usbserial-A9014TM4                                                    Send

Connection: close
Set-Cookie: __cfduid=df5cd887f8e3d2f80708f8928cb75b10e1456302644; expires=Thu, 23-Feb-17 08:30:44 GMT
X-Powered-By: Bitcoin Love
Cache-Control: max-age=15
Expires: Wed, 24 Feb 2016 08:31:07 UTC
X-BE: stinger
X-Proxy-Cache: HIT
Access-Control-Allow-Origin: *
X-Cache-Status-A: HIT
Server: cloudflare-nginx
CF-RAY: 2799cf6757982b09-WAW

{"time":{"updated":"Feb 24, 2016 08:30:00 UTC","updatedISO":"2016-02-24T08:30:00+00:00","updateduk":"

JSON answer:
{"time":{"updated":"Feb 24, 2016 08:30:00 UTC","updatedISO":"2016-02-24T08:30:00+00:00","updateduk":"

Bitcoin price:
416.45

☐ Autoscroll                                    Both NL & CR  ⬍   115200 baud  ⬍
```

As you can see, the price when I tested this project was 416.45 USD for one Bitcoin. Of course, you should also see this information on the OLED screen:

Congratulations, you just made your own physical Bitcoin ticker!

Adding alert LEDs to the ticker

We did the hardest project so far: we built a physical Bitcoin ticker that indicates the price of Bitcoin in real time.

We're now ready to add little improvements to the project to make it even better. For example, we are going to add two LEDs, one red and one green, to indicate whether the Bitcoin price is going up or down.

We are going to flash the red LED when the price is going down, and the green one when it's going up.

But first, we need to add the hardware to the project. Simply place the LEDs in series with the 330 Ohm resistors on the breadboard, and then connect them as we saw in earlier chapters. Make sure to connect the red LED to pin 5, and the green LED to pin 4, of the ESP8266 board.

This is the final result for this part:

Let's now see how to configure this project. I will only detail here what changed compared to the previous project:

1. We first need to define the pins to which the LEDs are connected:

   ```
   #define LED_PIN_UP 4
   #define LED_PIN_DOWN 5
   ```

2. Then, we define a variable to store the previous value of the price, and also a threshold (in USD) on which we'll flash the LED:

   ```
   floatpreviousValue = 0.0;
   float threshold = 0.05;
   ```

3. In the `setup()` function of the sketch, we set the LED pins as outputs:

   ```
   pinMode(LED_PIN_DOWN, OUTPUT);
   pinMode(LED_PIN_UP, OUTPUT);
   ```

4. Inside the `loop()` function, we first check whether it's the first time we are running the code. If yes, we set the previous value to the current Bitcoin price:

   ```
   if (previousValue == 0.0) {
   previousValue = price;
     }
   ```

5. Then, we check whether the price went down by at least the threshold amount. If that's the case, we flash the red LED:

   ```
   if (price < (previousValue - threshold)) {

       // Flash LED
   digitalWrite(LED_PIN_DOWN, HIGH);
   delay(100);
   digitalWrite(LED_PIN_DOWN, LOW);
   delay(100);
   digitalWrite(LED_PIN_DOWN, HIGH);
   delay(100);
   digitalWrite(LED_PIN_DOWN, LOW);


     }
   ```

6. We then do the same for the green LED when the price goes up:

```
if (price > (previousValue + threshold)) {

    // Flash LED
digitalWrite(LED_PIN_UP, HIGH);
delay(100);
digitalWrite(LED_PIN_UP, LOW);
delay(100);
digitalWrite(LED_PIN_UP, HIGH);
delay(100);
digitalWrite(LED_PIN_UP, LOW);

}
```

7. Finally, we set the previous price to the current price:

```
previousValue = price;
```

Again, let's try the project. You will find the code inside the GitHub repository for the book. Then, upload the code to the board. You should see immediately that whenever the price goes up or down (beyond the thresholds), one of the LEDs should quickly flash.

Summary

Let's summarize what we achieved in this project. We used the ESP8266 Wi-Fi chip to grab the price of Bitcoin from a web API, and we displayed this price on an OLED screen connected to the ESP8266. Then, we also added two LEDs to the project to check whether the price is going up or down.

You can of course do many other things with this project. You can, for example, display the price of Bitcoin in currencies other than USD, and implement a switch button to change the display currency.

In the next chapter, we are going to see how to use the ESP8266 to monitor and, if required, water a plant (or a whole garden!) from the cloud.

10
Wireless Gardening with the ESP8266

In this chapter, we are again going to take everything we've learned so far and apply it to a concrete project. Here, we are going to building a wireless, cloud-based gardening project based on the ESP8266. It will allow you to monitor the temperature and humidity of a plant, or your whole garden, and water it if necessary.

We are first going to set up the project so it sends you automated alerts when the plant is dry. Then, we'll set it up so you can not only monitor it remotely, but also activate a watering pump if necessary. Let's start!

Hardware and software requirements

Apart from the ESP8266WiFi chip, the core requirement of this chapter is the temperature and humidity sensor. As we will actually stick this sensor into the ground, we can't use the usual sensors we used earlier in this book.

Therefore, we need to use a sensor that is appropriate to be inserted into the soil. This is the case for the sensor I will use for this project, sold by Adafruit and based on the SHT10 sensor from Sensirion:

To use the sensor with the ESP8266WiFi chip, you will also need a 10K Ohm resistor.

You will also need a way to water the plant or your garden if necessary. For this, I simply used the 5V relay that we already used earlier in this chapter. This way, you can simply control most of the water pumps you can find on the market.

As usual, you'll also need a breadboard and jumper wires.

This is a list of all the components that will be used in this chapter:

- AdafruitES8266 module (https://www.adafruit.com/products/2471)
- FTDI USB module (https://www.adafruit.com/products/284)
- Soil moisture sensor (https://www.adafruit.com/products/1298)
- 5V relay module (https://www.pololu.com/product/2480)
- 10K Ohm resistor (https://www.sparkfun.com/products/8374)
- Breadboard (https://www.sparkfun.com/products/12002)
- Jumper wires (https://www.sparkfun.com/products/9194)

On the software side, you will need the library for the SHT10 sensor, which you can download from here:

https://github.com/practicalarduino/SHT1x

Hardware configuration

We are now going to assemble the different parts of this project. First, you need to get familiar with the different pins of the SHT10 sensor:

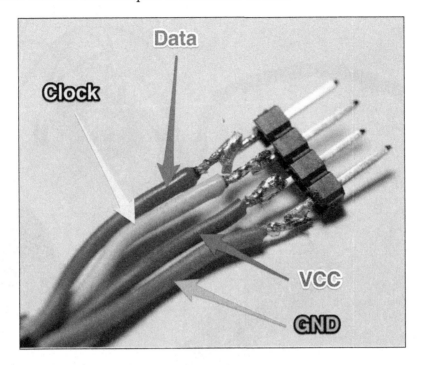

Once that's done, put the sensor's connector on the breadboard. Also connect the VCC and GND pins of the ESP8266 to the breadboard red and blue power lines.

Next, connect the sensor's VCC and GND pins to the red and blue power rails, respectively. Then, connect the data pin to pin number 4 of the ESP8266, and the clock pin to pin number 5. Finally, add the 10K Ohm pull-up resistor between the data and the VCC pins of the sensor.

For the relay, simply connect GND to the blue power rail, VCC to the red one, and finally the SIG pin to pin number 15 of the ESP8266.

This is the final result:

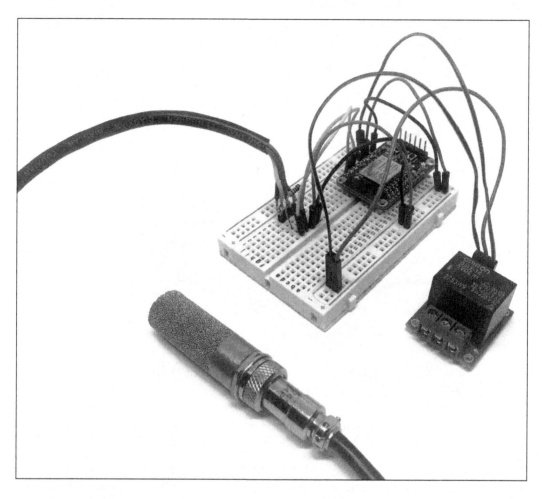

However, we are not done yet; we need something to measure! You can now insert the sensor inside the soil, for example in the pot of a plant inside your home, or in your garden outside. This is how I inserted it to monitor one of the plants in my home:

Creating alerts to water your plant

Before creating all the exciting wireless gardening projects you'll find in this chapter, we are going to start with one important thing: testing whether the sensor is working properly!

For that, here is the sketch to check that the sensor is functioning correctly:

```
// Library
#include <SHT1x.h>

// Pins
#define dataPin  4
#define clockPin 5

// Create instance for the sensor
SHT1xsht1x(dataPin, clockPin);
```

```
void setup()
{
Serial.begin(115200); // Open serial connection to report values to
host
Serial.println("Starting up");
}

void loop()
{
   // Variables
float temp_c;
float temp_f;
float humidity;

   // Read values from the sensor
temp_c = sht1x.readTemperatureC();
temp_f = sht1x.readTemperatureF();
humidity = sht1x.readHumidity();

   // Print the values to the serial port
Serial.print("Temperature: ");
Serial.print(temp_c, DEC);
Serial.print("C / ");
Serial.print(temp_f, DEC);
Serial.print("F. Humidity: ");
Serial.print(humidity);
Serial.println("%");

   // Wait 2 seconds
delay(2000);
}
```

This sketch is pretty straightforward: we create an instance of the SHT library, and in the loop() function we just make measurements and print the results on the Serial monitor.

Just copy this sketch inside the Arduino IDE, put the ESP8266 in bootloader mode, and upload the code to the board. Then, open the **Serial** monitor. This is what you should see inside the **Serial** monitor:

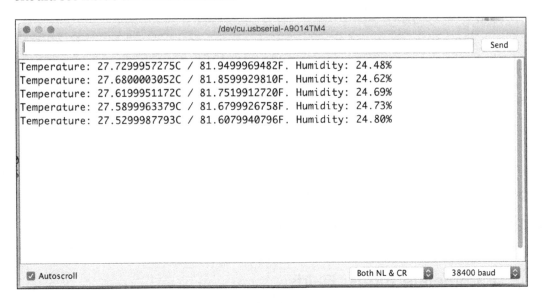

If you have values that make sense (temperature around room temperature, for example), it means your sensor is working properly. If not, please check all the connections again, and make sure that you inserted the 10K Ohm resistor between the data and VCC pins of the sensor. For me, this is what made the sensor not work during the first trial.

Now, we are going to set up automated alerts on our phone whenever the plant is getting too dry. The first step to do that is to create an account at IFTTT, which we already used earlier in the book:

```
https://ifttt.com/
```

I will also assume that you already have a **Maker** and **Pushover** channels. If not, please refer to *Chapter 6, Machine-to-Machine Communications*, in which we already used IFTTT.

Next, create a new recipe with the Maker channel:

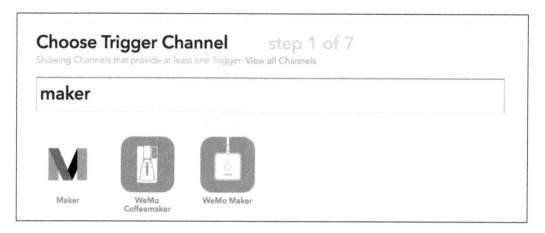

You need to insert **alert** as the event name:

For the target channel, we'll use Pushover to receive notifications on your mobile device:

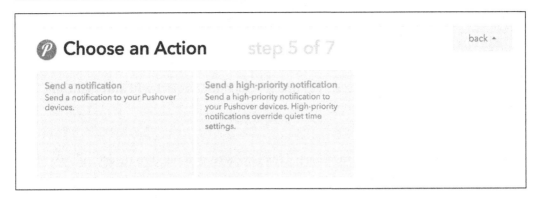

Now, insert a message inside the notification message field:

Once the recipe is created, we need to actually configure the board so it automatically sends alerts whenever the humidity of the plant is getting too low. As the code is quite complex here, I will only highlight the most important points. It starts by including the correct libraries:

```
#include <ESP8266WiFi.h>
#include <SHT1x.h>
```

Then, we need to define your Wi-Fi name and password:

```
const char* ssid = "wifi-name";
const char* password = "wifi-pass";
```

We also define a humidity threshold, under which the project will automatically send an alert:

```
float threshold = 30.00;
```

Next, we define the IFTTT parameters. This is where you need to insert the key of your IFTTT Maker channel:

```
const char* host = "maker.ifttt.com";
const char* eventName  = "alert";
const char* key = "ifttt-key";
```

In the loop() function of the sketch, after taking the measurements from the sensor, we check whether the humidity is below the threshold:

```
if (humidity < threshold) {
```

If that's the case, we prepare the request we'll send to the IFTTT server:

```
String url = "/trigger/";
url += eventName;
url += "/with/key/";
url += key;
```

We then send this request:

```
client.print(String("GET ") + url + " HTTP/1.1\r\n" +
             "Host: " + host + "\r\n" +
             "Connection: close\r\n\r\n");
int timeout = millis() + 5000;
while (client.available() == 0) {
if (timeout - millis() < 0) {
Serial.println(">>> Client Timeout !");
client.stop();
return;
    }
  }
```

If the request is sent, we also wait a long time before the next alert, to not continuously receive alerts from the project:

```
delay(10 * 60 * 1000);
```

It's now time to test this first project of the chapter! Make sure to grab the complete code and modify the credentials, such as the IFTTT settings. Then, upload the code to the board. If the humidity is indeed below the threshold, you will soon receive a notification on your phone stating that the plant needs to be watered:

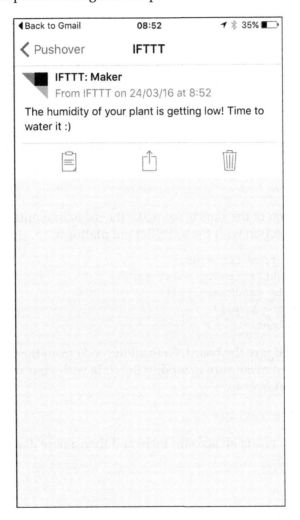

Monitoring the temperature and humidity

In this second project of the chapter, we are going to do something different. We will monitor the temperature and humidity of the plant from the cloud dashboard that we already used earlier in the chapter. We are first going to configure the board, and then set up the cloud dashboard.

As we already saw how to use the aREST cloud platform earlier in the book, I will only highlight the most important parts of the code.

The first step is to include all the required libraries, including the aREST library:

```
#include <ESP8266WiFi.h>
#include <PubSubClient.h>
#include <aREST.h>
#include <SHT1x.h>
```

Then, we give an ID to our device:

```
char* device_id = "gveie2y5";
```

As usual, you also need to put your Wi-Fi name and password here:

```
const char* ssid = "your-wifi";
const char* password = "your-password";
```

In the `loop()` function of the sketch, we make the measurements from the sensor, and handle the connection with the aREST cloud platform:

```
// Read values from the sensor
temperature = sht1x.readTemperatureC();
humidity = sht1x.readHumidity();
// Connect to the cloud
rest.handle(client);
```

It is now time to configure the board. Grab all the code from the GitHub repository for the book, and then make sure to modify the code with your own credentials and device ID. Then, head over to:

```
http://dashboard.arest.io/
```

If that's not done yet, create an account there and then a new dashboard:

Inside this newly created dashboard, create a new variable indicator with the following parameters:

You should immediately see a live measurement coming from the board:

Then, repeat the same step for the humidity measurement:

Temperature	22.42	gardening	ONLINE	Delete
Humidity	17.12	gardening	ONLINE	Delete

You can now monitor the temperature and humidity of your plant or garden, from anywhere in the world.

But we are still missing one key element: the pump. Wouldn't it be great to also be able to activate the water pump remotely when you see that the humidity is going down? Or even to have it automatically activated when the humidity is too low? This is what we are going to see in the next part of this chapter.

Automating your gardening

We are now going to configure our project so it automatically waters the plant if the humidity falls below a given threshold.

The first step is actually to define two thresholds:

```
floatlowThreshold = 20.00;
floathighThreshold = 25.00;
```

We need two thresholds here because if we just defined one, the pump will constantly switch between the on and off states.

So we will have the pump turn on when the humidity goes below the low threshold, and turn off when we reach the high threshold again.

Next, we define which pin the relay is connected to:

```
#define relayPin 15
```

In the `setup()` function of the sketch, we set the relay pin as an output:

```
pinMode(relayPin, OUTPUT);
```

In the `loop()` function, we constantly check whether the humidity went below the low threshold, or above the high threshold:

```
if (humidity <lowThreshold) {

// Activate pump
digitalWrite(relayPin, HIGH);

}

if (humidity >highThreshold) {

// Deactivate pump
digitalWrite(relayPin, LOW);

}
```

I only highlighted the most important parts of the code here, but you can of course grab the complete code from the GitHub repository for the book. Now, get the code and modify it with your own credentials. Then, upload the code to the board.

Once that's done, go back to the dashboard you created before. You can now add another element for the pump, with the following set of parameters:

You should immediately see the buttons appear, with the current status of the relay:

Gardening						Show Edit Mode
Temperature		22.94		gardening	ONLINE	
Humidity		16.8		gardening	ONLINE	
Pump	On	Off	LOW	gardening	ONLINE	

You can now try it; press the **On** button, and the pump should immediately turn on:

Gardening						Show Edit Mode
Temperature		22.94		gardening	ONLINE	
Humidity		16.8		gardening	ONLINE	
Pump	On	Off	HIGH	gardening	ONLINE	

You should also notice that any time the humidity drops below the threshold, it should immediately activate the pump, until the humidity reaches the high threshold again.

Summary

In this chapter, we saw how to build a cloud gardening project based on the ESP8266WiFi chip. You learned how to create alerts for your plants or garden, how to monitor them from anywhere, and how to make sure the water pump is automatically activated when the humidity gets too low.

You can of course take what you learned in this chapter and go much further with it. It would, for example, be really easy to just add more units to the project, and monitor several plants at once in different locations.

In the next chapter, we are going to build yet another project using what we learned so far about the ESP8266: a complete home automation system that we will control and monitor from the cloud.

11

Cloud-Based Home Automation System

In this chapter, we are going to use everything we learned so far in the book, and apply it to the home automation field. We are going to build a simple but complete home automation system that we will completely control from the cloud, thanks to the ESP8266 Wi-Fi chip. The system will be composed of a motion sensor, a temperature and humidity sensor, and an LED dimmer. This way, it will mimic all the essential components of a real home automation system.

We are going to build three projects based on this system. We are first going to see how to simply control every component of the system using an online dashboard. Then, we are going to see how to send automated alarms to your phone when motion is detected in your home. Finally, we are going to see how to automate your home using IFTTT and the system we created. Let's start!

Hardware and software requirements

Let's first see what we need for this project. You will mainly need components we already used in previous chapters, such as the ESP8266 module, an LED, and the DHT11 sensor.

The only new component here is a PIR motion sensor that we will use to detect motion in our home. I used a simple 5V-compatible PIR motion sensor, which is a pretty standard component.

I listed all the components for this chapter, based on one motion sensor module, one LED dimmer, and one sensor module. Of course, if you want to use more of each module, this is no problem, you just need to add more ESP8266 modules to the project.

This is a list of all the components that will be used in this chapter:

- Adafruit ES8266 module (x3) (https://www.adafruit.com/products/2471)
- FTDI USB module (https://www.adafruit.com/products/284)
- DHT11 sensor (https://www.adafruit.com/products/386)
- LED (https://www.sparkfun.com/products/9590)
- 330 Ohm resistor (https://www.sparkfun.com/products/8377)
- PIR motion sensor (https://www.sparkfun.com/products/13285)
- Breadboard (x3) (https://www.sparkfun.com/products/12002)
- Jumper wires (x3) (https://www.sparkfun.com/products/9194)

On the software side, you will need the aREST library, the PubSub library, and also the DHT sensor library. We already installed those libraries in previous chapters of the book, but if that's not done yet, you can simply install them using the Arduino IDE library manager.

Hardware configuration

We are now going to assemble the different parts of this project. First, we are going to configure the motion sensor module. For this first module, after placing the ESP8266 board on the breadboard, connect the VCC pin of the sensor to VCC, GND to GND, and finally the OUT pin of the sensor to pin number 5 of the ESP8266.

This is the final result for this module:

Let's now deal with the temperature and humidity module. Place the sensor on the breadboard, and then connect the first pin to VCC, the second pin to pin number 5 of the ESP8266 board, and finally the last pin of the sensor to GND.

This is the final result for this module:

Let's now assemble the LED dimmer module. Here, we are going to use a simple LED as the output, but you can of course use this as the starting point of a module to control more LEDs in your home, or even lamps.

To connect the LED to the ESP8266, simply place the LED in series with the 330 Ohm resistor on the breadboard, the longest pin of the LED in contact with the resistor. Then, connect the other end of the resistor to pin 5 of the ESP8266, and connect the other end of the LED to GND.

This is the final result for this module:

Controlling your home from a dashboard

In the first project of this chapter, we are going to learn how to control all the modules we assembled before from a cloud dashboard, using the aREST framework we already used in this book.

First, let's configure all the modules. We are going to start with the LED dimmer module, which is the easiest to configure. Here is the complete code for this module:

```
// Import required libraries
#include "ESP8266WiFi.h"
#include <PubSubClient.h>
```

```
#include <aREST.h>

// Clients
WiFiClient espClient;
PubSubClient client(espClient);

// Unique ID to identify the device for cloud.arest.io
char* device_id = "6g37g4";

// Create aREST instance
aREST rest = aREST(client);

// WiFi parameters
const char* ssid = "wifi-name";
const char* password = "wifi-pass";

// The port to listen for incoming TCP connections
#define LISTEN_PORT             80

// Create an instance of the server
WiFiServer server(LISTEN_PORT);

void setup(void)
{
  // Start Serial
  Serial.begin(115200);

  // Set callback
  client.setCallback(callback);

  // Give name and ID to device
  rest.set_id(device_id);
  rest.set_name("dimmer");

  // Connect to WiFi
  WiFi.begin(ssid, password);
  while (WiFi.status() != WL_CONNECTED) {
    delay(500);
    Serial.print(".");
  }
  Serial.println("");
  Serial.println("WiFi connected");
```

```
    // Start the server
    server.begin();
    Serial.println("Server started");

    // Print the IP address
    Serial.println(WiFi.localIP());

}

void loop() {

    // Handle REST calls
    rest.handle(client);

}

// Handles message arrived on subscribed topic(s)
void callback(char* topic, byte* payload, unsigned int length) {

    // Handle
    rest.handle_callback(client, topic, payload, length);

}
```

There are several things you need to modify in this code. You need to substitute the Wi-Fi name and password for your own. You also need to modify the device ID of the device, so it has a unique identifier on the network. Finally, you can also modify the name of the device, for example to add some data about where the module is located in your home.

Once that's all done, upload the code to the board, and then move on to the next device: the motion sensor.

For this module, the code is nearly the same, we just need to add some lines to constantly measure the state of the motion sensor and make it available on the cloud. For that, we first define a variable that will host the motion sensor state:

```
    int motion;
```

Then, we expose this variable to aREST:

```
    rest.variable("motion", &motion);
```

Next, inside the `loop()` function of the sketch, we simply measure the state of the motion sensor:

```
motion = digitalRead(5);
```

After modifying the same parameters as for the LED module (Wi-Fi credentials, device ID, and name), upload the code to the board.

Finally, let's deal with the sensor module. For this one, you will need to import the DHT library:

```
#include "DHT.h"
```

Then, you will need to define which pin the sensor is connected to:

```
#define DHTPIN 5
#define DHTTYPE DHT11
```

After that, create an instance of the sensor:

```
DHT dht(DHTPIN, DHTTYPE, 15);
```

We also create two variables that will hold the value of the measured temperature and humidity:

```
float temperature;
float humidity;
```

In the `setup()` function of the sketch, we initialize the DHT sensor:

```
dht.begin();
```

We also expose those variables to the aREST API:

```
rest.variable("temperature",&temperature);
rest.variable("humidity",&humidity);
```

Finally, inside the `loop()` function of the sketch, we measure the temperature and humidity of the sensor:

```
humidity = dht.readHumidity();
temperature = dht.readTemperature();
```

Again, modify the required parameters inside the sketch and upload it to the board. Note that to power all the modules, you can, for example, use either an external battery or a breadboard power supply; you do not need to have one FTDI cable per module.

It's now time to control all our boards from the cloud! First, go over to the aREST dashboard website:

`http://dashboard.arest.io/`

Create a new dashboard for your home automation system:

Inside this dashboard, switch to edit mode and add the first element that will hold the temperature measurement. Make sure to enter the correct ID of your temperature and humidity module:

Next, do the same for humidity, and you should get the following result:

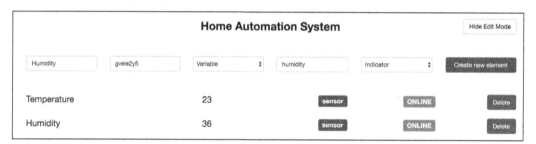

We are now going to add the LED dimmer module. As we want to be able to control the intensity of the LED light, create a new element with the **Analog** option:

You should now be able to control the intensity of the LED via a slider inside the dashboard:

Finally, create a new element for the motion sensor:

You should end up with a dashboard that has all the elements of the simple home automation system we just built:

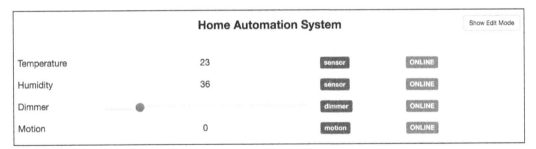

Congratulations, you just built a complete home automation system based on the ESP8266, which you can now control from the cloud. You can of course add more modules to the system, and control them from the same dashboard.

 Note that as this dashboard is accessible from anywhere, you don't actually need to be inside your home to access it!

Creating a cloud alarm system

We are now going to build another project based on the same hardware we have already built in this chapter. This time, we are going to make an alarm system based in the cloud, using the ESP8266 module along with the PIR motion sensor.

I will show you how to do it with just one PIR sensor, but you can of course add more modules that will be dispersed around your home or any building you wish to monitor. To do that, we are going to again use IFTTT, which will send you a text message every time motion is detected by any of the motion sensor modules.

Let's first see how to configure a given module. As it's code that is very similar to what we already saw earlier in this book, I will only highlight the most important parts here.

You need to set the key that is linked to your **Maker** channel on IFTTT:

```
const char* host = "maker.ifttt.com";
const char* eventName  = "motion_detected";
const char* key = "key";
```

Then, inside the loop() function of the sketch, we read the status of the motion sensor:

```
bool motion = digitalRead(5);
```

We then check whether any motion was detected:

```
if (motion) {
```

If that is the case, we build a request that we will send to IFTTT:

```
String url = "/trigger/";
    url += eventName;
    url += "/with/key/";
    url += key;
```

We then actually send this request to the IFTTT servers:

```
client.print(String("GET ") + url + " HTTP/1.1\r\n" +
                "Host: " + host + "\r\n" +
                "Connection: close\r\n\r\n");
    int timeout = millis() + 5000;
    while (client.available() == 0) {
      if (timeout - millis() < 0) {
```

```
        Serial.println(">>> Client Timeout !");
        client.stop();
        return;
    }
}
```

After that, we read the answer:

```
while(client.available()){
    String line = client.readStringUntil('\r');
    Serial.print(line);
}
```

We then wait for a long time before sending new alerts; otherwise we'll just send a lot of messages to your mobile phone:

```
delay(10 * 60 * 1000);
```

Now, grab the code (for example from the GitHub repository for the book), modify it with your own credentials, and upload it to the board.

Now, head over to IFTTT to create a new recipe:

```
https://ifttt.com/
```

As the trigger channel, select the **Maker** channel:

Choose Trigger Channel   step 1 of 7

Showing Channels that provide at least one Trigger. View all Channels

maker

Maker

WeMo
Coffeemaker

WeMo Maker

As the event, insert `motion_detected`, which is also what we put in the code:

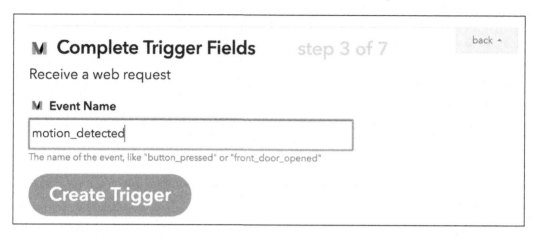

As the action channel, we'll select **SMS** here, as it will be the fastest way to contact you in case an alarm is triggered by your motion sensor:

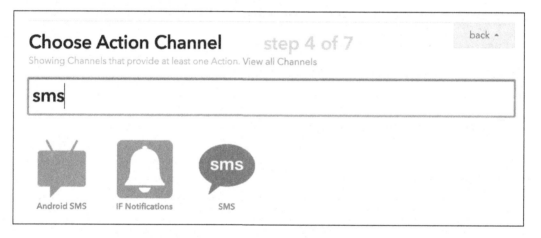

You can insert whatever you wish as the message, for example:

Now, create the recipe and activate it. You should see that whenever you pass your hand in front of the sensor, it will almost immediately send an alert message to your phone. If you wish to stop your alarm system, it's then as simple as deactivating the recipe on IFTTT.

You can of course add more sensors to the system, making each publish the same alert on IFTTT. Therefore, whenever any sensor detects motion, you will receive an alert on your phone.

Automating your home

In the last part of this chapter, we are going to play a bit more with IFTTT. This time, instead of using the motion sensor, we'll see how to use the different trigger channels of IFTTT to create nice automation flows to control the LED module. Of course, remember that you could replace the LED with any appliance you wish to control, for example a lamp.

The **Maker** channel of IFTTT can also be used as an action channel, and this is what we are going to use here. We will use it to call the aREST API whenever a given condition is triggered.

We are first going to configure the module again, so it can receive commands from the cloud. This is the part of the code before the `setup()` function:

```
// Import required libraries
#include "ESP8266WiFi.h"
#include <PubSubClient.h>
#include <aREST.h>

// Clients
WiFiClient espClient;
PubSubClient client(espClient);

// Unique ID to identify the device for cloud.arest.io
char* device_id = "6g37g4";

// Create aREST instance
aREST rest = aREST(client);

// WiFi parameters
const char* ssid = "wifi-name";
const char* password = "wifi-pass";

// The port to listen for incoming TCP connections
#define LISTEN_PORT          80

// Create an instance of the server
WiFiServer server(LISTEN_PORT);
```

This is the `setup()` function of the code:

```
void setup(void)
{
  // Start Serial
  Serial.begin(115200);

  // Set callback
  client.setCallback(callback);

  // Give name and ID to device
  rest.set_id(device_id);
  rest.set_name("dimmer");
```

```
  // Connect to WiFi
  WiFi.begin(ssid, password);
  while (WiFi.status() != WL_CONNECTED) {
    delay(500);
    Serial.print(".");
  }
  Serial.println("");
  Serial.println("WiFi connected");

  // Start the server
  server.begin();
  Serial.println("Server started");

  // Print the IP address
  Serial.println(WiFi.localIP());

  // LED pin to output
  pinMode(5, OUTPUT);

}
```

Finally, here is the `loop()` function of the code:

```
void loop() {

  // Handle REST calls
  rest.handle(client);

}

// Handles message arrived on subscribed topic(s)
void callback(char* topic, byte* payload, unsigned int length) {

  // Handle
  rest.handle_callback(client, topic, payload, length);

}
```

Now, modify the important credentials (Wi-Fi name and password, and device ID) in the code, and upload it to the board.

Then, go back to IFTTT. The first thing we are going to do is to make a project to light up the LED at a given time (for example, when it's becoming dark outside), and then it off again at another time (for example, when you go to bed).

For that, create a new recipe with **Date & Time** as the channel. You might need to connect it first if you have never used it before:

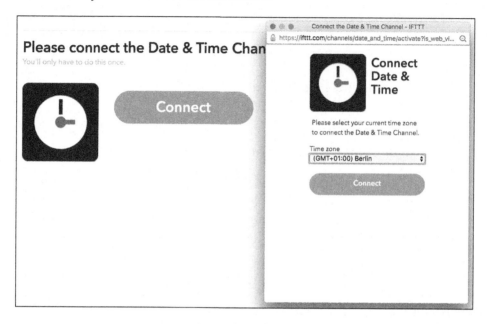

For the trigger type, select **Every day**, and enter the time at which you want the LED to turn on.

Then, for the action channel in IFTTT, select the **Maker** channel, and then select **Make a web request**. This will allow IFTTT to send a command to the aREST.io cloud server.

As the request, enter the following parameters, of course changing the device ID with the one you used inside the sketch:

Now, do the same with the time you want the LED to turn off, for example at 11.30 PM:

Choose the same action channel as earlier:

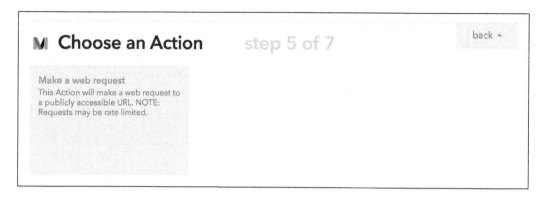

For the web request, enter the same parameters as before, but this time with the command to switch pin number 5 to LOW:

Now, validate the recipe:

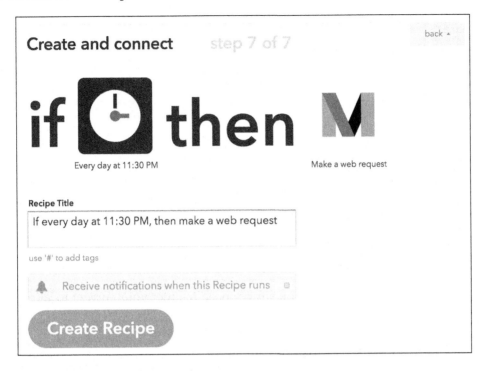

It's now time to see the recipe in action! Make sure the ESP8266 board is correctly configured, and also that the recipes are activated in IFTTT. Whenever the time conditions are met, you should immediately see the LED turn on or off. You can, of course, modify the times inside the recipes to test them.

Now, let's play with another trigger channel to see how powerful IFTTT is. You can, for example, use the **Weather** channel to check whether it's sunset, to automatically turn on the LED at this time without having to enter a fixed time.

To do so, create a new recipe and select the Weather channel, which you need to connect to:

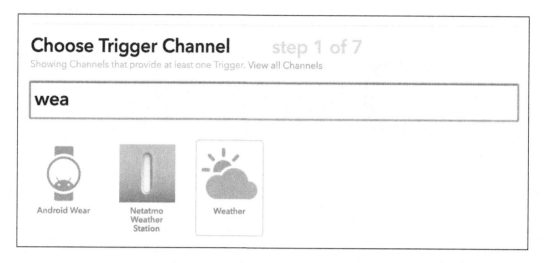

To connect the Weather channel, you simply need to enter your current location:

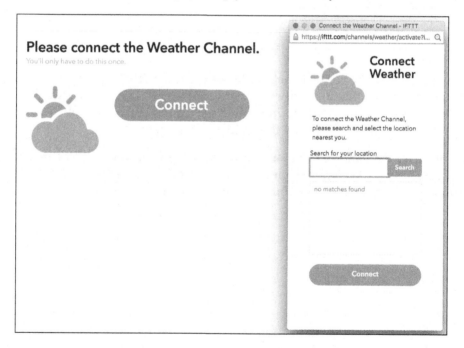

As the trigger type, I chose to trigger the even at sunset:

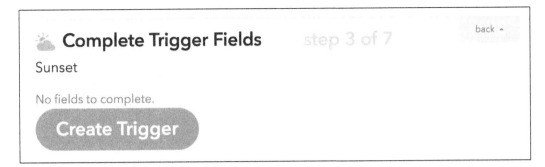

As the action channel, I selected the Maker channel, as I did earlier:

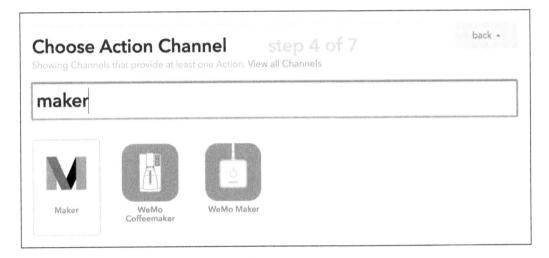

Also, just as in the previous recipe, I decided to turn the LED on whenever the recipe is triggered:

You can now see the newly created recipe:

You should now see that whenever sunset approaches, the LED will automatically turn on. You can of course play with more conditions inside IFTTT, and even use the Maker channel as both the trigger and the action channel, to link the different modules of your home automation system via IFTTT.

Summary

In this chapter, we built the different components of a home automation system based on the ESP8266, and we saw how to control everything from the cloud. We first created a cloud dashboard to control all the devices from a single interface. Next, we used IFTTT again to create an alarm system that automatically sends you alerts on your phone whenever motion is detected. The easiest way to build your own system based on this project is to simply add more modules, so it suits the needs you have in your own home. For example, it is really easy to add several motion sensor modules so you can have a complete alarm system deployed in your home, and that you can manage using a simple web browser.

In the next chapter, we are going to use the ESP8266 for a completely different application: building a mobile robot that we will control from the cloud.

12
Cloud-Controlled ESP8266 Robot

In this book so far, we mainly used the ESP8266 Wi-Fi chip to build Internet of Things projects that were related to the home automation or security fields, such as the remote-controlled door lock, or the complete home automation system we built in *Chapter 11, Cloud-Based Home Automation System*.

However, the ESP8266 is a very versatile chip, and can be used for several fields other than the two I cited above. For example, it can also be used as the "brain" of a mobile robot, and this is exactly what we are going to do in this chapter.

We are going to build a small mobile robot that will be completely controlled by the ESP8266 Wi-Fi chip. We are going to connect the motors of the robot to the ESP8266 Wi-Fi chip, and then the chip will communicate wirelessly with a cloud platform, so the robot can be controlled from anywhere. Finally, we are going to control the robot from a cloud dashboard. Let's start!

Hardware and software requirements

The first thing we need for this project is the ESP8266 Wi-Fi chip. As for most of this book, I will be using the Adafruit Huzzah ESP8266 board here.

Then, the other important component for this project will be the robot platform. There are many options on the market, but there are actually not so many that are made for the ESP8266, so we will need to choose a very generic platform that we can just mount the components of our choosing on.

We basically need a certain amount of features to have a robot platform for this project:

- The platform needs to have at least two wheels
- The platform needs to have two motors
- The platforms needs to be big enough to host the ESP8266, a breadboard, and batteries

There are actually a large number of robot platforms that would work with those specifications. The first category is of course the simple two-wheeled robot kits, such as this kit from EmGreat:

These platforms just have two wheels with a motor on each, and then a free wheel on the front to make the robot stable. Then, you can just mount your hardware on top of it.

Then, you have four-wheeled robots that are basically a little car on which you can mount your own hardware. This is the four-wheeled kit of the same brand as before:

 If you are going for such a platform, make sure there are only two motors, as in this chapter I will describe a project using two motors only. Of course, you could also easily adapt the code in this chapter to a four-motor robot platform.

I made a similar choice for this chapter, as I still had a rover-type robot I wanted to use:

This is basically the same as the robot I introduced earlier, but this time with rubber bands around the wheels, like a tank. This makes sure that the robot won't be too affected by what's behind it, such as some asperities on the ground. It also has only two motors.

After that, you will need additional components to control the robot. The first thing is the L293D chip, which is an integrated circuit specialized in motor control. Indeed, it would be impossible to directly control the motors from the ESP8266.

You will also need a battery that is adapted to the motors of your robot platform. The motors of the rover chassis I am using were rated for 7V, so I used this 7.4V battery:

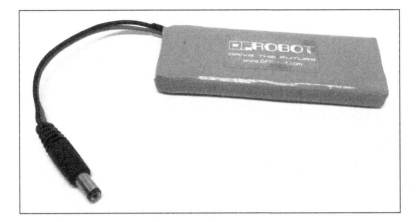

You will also need the usual breadboard and jumper wires.

This is a list of all the components that will be used in this chapter:

- Adafruit ES8266 module (`https://www.adafruit.com/products/2471`)
- FTDI USB module (`https://www.adafruit.com/products/284`)
- Rover robot chassis with two motors (`http://www.dfrobot.com/index.php?route=product/product&product_id=390`)
- L293D motor driver (`https://www.adafruit.com/products/807`)
- 7.4V battery URL with DC jack (`http://www.robotshop.com/en/dfrobot-7-4v-lipo-2200mah-battery.html`)
- Breadboard (`https://www.sparkfun.com/products/12002`)
- Jumper wires (`https://www.sparkfun.com/products/9194`)

On the software side, you will need the Arduino IDE and the aREST library that we already used earlier in the book.

Hardware configuration

We are now going to assemble the project. As it is quite complicated, I made a detailed diagram for you to understand the different connections:

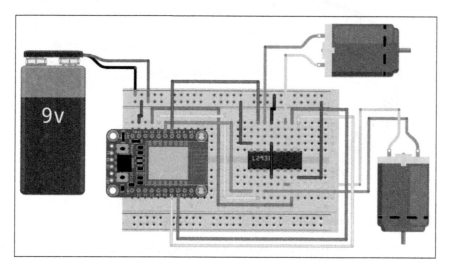

To help you out, I also created a detailed schematic:

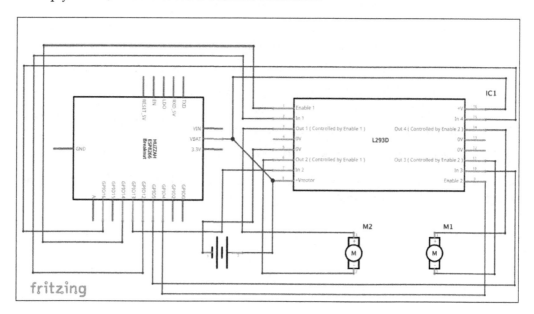

The first step is to assemble all the components on the breadboard. Only then place the breadboard on the robot chassis, and then connect it to the motors. At the end, connect the battery to the project.

This is the final result, only showing the breadboard, without all the connections to the motors:

This is the completely assembled robot platform:

Note that the platform comes with a cover to hide the components inside, but here I decided to leave it open so you can see the inside of the project. But don't do this with your own robot, or make sure to screw/glue all the components to the chassis!

Testing the motors

Before we actually control the robot from the cloud, we are going to perform a simple test to see whether the motors are working correctly. This will also allow you to see how to write code to control the motors.

This is the complete sketch for this part:

```
// Define motor pins
int motorOnePlus = 12;
int motorOneMinus = 13;
int motorOneEnable = 14;

int motorTwoPlus = 5;
int motorTwoMinus = 16;
int motorTwoEnable = 4;

void setup()
{

    Serial.begin(1152000);

    // Set pins
    pinMode(motorOnePlus, OUTPUT);
    pinMode(motorOneMinus, OUTPUT);
    pinMode(motorOneEnable, OUTPUT);

    pinMode(motorTwoPlus, OUTPUT);
    pinMode(motorTwoMinus, OUTPUT);
    pinMode(motorTwoEnable, OUTPUT);

}

void loop()
{

    // Accelerate forward
    setMotorOne(true, 500);
    setMotorTwo(true, 500);

    // Delay
    delay(5000);

    // Stop
    setMotorOne(true, 0);
    setMotorTwo(true, 0);
```

```
    // Delay
    delay(5000);

}

// Function to control the motor
void setMotorOne(boolean forward, int motor_speed){
    digitalWrite(motorOnePlus, forward);
    digitalWrite(motorOneMinus, !forward);
    analogWrite(motorOneEnable, motor_speed);
}

// Function to control the motor
void setMotorTwo(boolean forward, int motor_speed){
    digitalWrite(motorTwoPlus, forward);
    digitalWrite(motorTwoMinus, !forward);
    analogWrite(motorTwoEnable, motor_speed);
}
```

We are now going to see the important parts of this code. First, we define all the pins we used to connect the ESP8266 to the L293D motor driver:

```
int motorOnePlus = 12;
int motorOneMinus = 13;
int motorOneEnable = 14;

int motorTwoPlus = 5;
int motorTwoMinus = 16;
int motorTwoEnable = 4;
```

In the setup() function of the sketch, we set all those pins as outputs:

```
pinMode(motorOnePlus, OUTPUT);
pinMode(motorOneMinus, OUTPUT);
pinMode(motorOneEnable, OUTPUT);

pinMode(motorTwoPlus, OUTPUT);
pinMode(motorTwoMinus, OUTPUT);
pinMode(motorTwoEnable, OUTPUT);
```

Inside the loop() function, we first set both motors to go forward at half of their maximum speed:

```
setMotorOne(true, 500);
setMotorTwo(true, 500);
```

Later, we also stop the motors, before starting them again. Let's now have a look at the function used to set the first motor:

```
void setMotorOne(boolean forward, int motor_speed){
    digitalWrite(motorOnePlus, forward);
  digitalWrite(motorOneMinus, !forward);
  analogWrite(motorOneEnable, motor_speed);
}
```

As you can see, there are two parts to this function: one part for the direction, and one part for the speed. The direction is set by applying two opposite logical signals on the + and – pins of the L293D, for this particular motor. For the speed, we just apply a PWM signal on the corresponding pin with an `analogWrite()` function. Note that the speed can be set from 0 to 1023 using this function.

The function to control the other motor is really similar:

```
void setMotorTwo(boolean forward, int motor_speed){
    digitalWrite(motorTwoPlus, forward);
    digitalWrite(motorTwoMinus, !forward);
    analogWrite(motorTwoEnable, motor_speed);
}
```

It's now time to test the sketch and to make the motors move! Before doing anything, make sure that the robot is standing on a little platform, so the wheels don't touch the ground. Otherwise you may get an unpleasant surprise when the wheels start to spin! Also check that the battery is connected to the robot.

Then, upload the code to the robot. You should see that the wheels will quickly start turning in the same direction, before stopping and then starting the loop again.

If the wheels are not turning in the same direction, make sure that all the connections are correct. This is important, as we want the robot to move forward when we apply the same command to both motors.

Connecting the robot to the cloud

Now that we are sure that the wheels are working correctly, we are going to connect the robot to the aREST cloud platform, so it can be controlled from anywhere in the world.

As the sketch is quite big and takes a lot from the motor test sketch we saw earlier, I will only go through the most important points here. You can of course find the complete sketch inside the GitHub repository for the book.

It starts by importing the correct libraries:

```
#include <ESP8266WiFi.h>
#include <PubSubClient.h>
#include <aREST.h>
```

Then, we create the client to communicate with the aREST cloud server:

```
WiFiClient espClient;
PubSubClient client(espClient);
```

We also create an instance of the aREST client:

```
aREST rest = aREST(client);
```

Then, as we saw in earlier chapters, you need to give a unique ID to the device:

```
char* device_id = "40ep12";
```

You also need to set your Wi-Fi name and password here:

```
const char* ssid = "wifi-name";
const char* password = "wifi-password";
```

Next, we need to define a set of functions to actually control the robot remotely. Here, I will use one function per fundamental command to the robot: stop, forward, backward, right, and left.

We first need to declare all those functions:

```
int stop(String command);
int forward(String command);
int left(String command);
int right(String command);
int backward(String command);
```

In the `setup()` function, we assign the ID to the board, and also give it a name:

```
rest.set_id(device_id);
rest.set_name("robot");
```

We need to expose the functions to the aREST library, so they can be called remotely:

```
rest.function("forward", forward);
rest.function("stop", stop);
rest.function("right", right);
rest.function("left", left);
rest.function("backward", backward);
```

After that, we connect the board to the Wi-Fi network:

```
WiFi.begin(ssid, password);
while (WiFi.status() != WL_CONNECTED) {
  delay(500);
  Serial.print(".");
}
Serial.println("");
Serial.println("WiFi connected");
```

In the `loop()` function, we connect to the cloud with this:

```
rest.handle(client);
```

Now, let's see one of those functions that we use to make the robot move around. This is the details of the function to make the robot move forward:

```
int forward(String command) {

  setMotorOne(true, 1000);
  setMotorTwo(true, 1000);


}
```

If you recall the functions from the previous section, this is just setting both motors to go in the same direction at (nearly) full speed.

It's now time to test the robot! Make sure that you grabbed the whole code from the GitHub repository of the book, assigned a unique ID to the project, and also changed the Wi-Fi credentials inside the code. Also make sure that the battery is connected to the robot.

Then, upload the code to the board. This time, after it's uploaded, nothing should happen. Now, to make the robot autonomous, disconnect it from the FTDI cable, and connect the Vbat pin to the battery power supply (the Adafruit ESP8266 chip can handle 7V without problems). If you have another ESP8266, you might need to power it from an external power source now.

Now, go to your favorite web browser and type:

```
https://cloud.arest.io/40ep12/id
```

Of course, you need to replace the ID with the one you set in the code. You should get the following answer:

```
{
    "id": "40ep12",
    "name": "robot",
    "connected": true
}
```

Then, make sure there is space around the robot and type:

```
https://cloud.arest.io/40ep12/forward
```

You should get the confirmation inside your browser that the function was executed, and you should also see the robot move forward! To stop it, simply type:

```
https://cloud.arest.io/40ep12/stop
```

This should immediately stop the robot. You can now also play with the other functions, to make the robot turn right or left, or go backwards. Congratulations, you can now control your robot from anywhere on the planet!

Controlling the robot from a dashboard

What we already achieved is great, but it's not perfect yet. It's not so convenient to control the robot from a web browser, especially to perform quick actions such as making the robot turn at a specific angle.

To easily control the robot, we are going to again use the dashboard functions of aREST, so we can control the robot using buttons.

If it's not been done yet, create an account at:

```
http://dashboard.arest.io/
```

From there, create a new dashboard for your robot:

Now, inside the newly created dashboard, we are going to create a button for the first function: going forward. To do so, create a new element with `function` as the type, and `forward` as the function to call:

Then, do the same for the stop function:

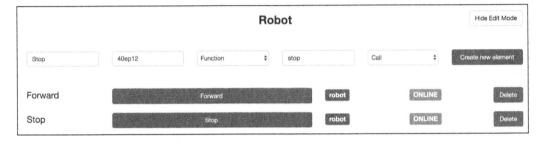

After that, do the same operation with all the remaining functions:

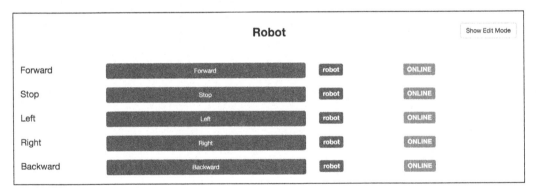

You can now immediately try the buttons; whenever you press a button, it should immediately perform the correct action on the ESP8266.

Summary

In this chapter, we used the ESP8266 for a completely different Internet of Things project from the other chapters: we built a mobile robot. The robot was directly connected to the cloud, and we used an online dashboard to control it with a graphical interface. The nice thing is that this can be used to control the robot from anywhere.

A nice way to improve this project would be to add sensors to it, and also manage those sensors from the cloud. You could, for example, add ultrasonic sensors to "see" what is in front of the robot.

In the next chapter, we are going to look at a more advanced topic: how to deploy you own cloud server, so you can have complete control over your Internet of Things project with the ESP8266.

13
Building Your Own Cloud Platform to Control ESP8266 Devices

In all the previous chapters of this book, we have always used external services to connect our ESP8266 projects to the cloud. For example, we used services such as IFTTT, Adafruit IO, and aREST to control and monitor our projects from the cloud.

However, those services are all managed by other people or companies. This can pose security issues for some projects, and also those services can be shut down at any time, or at least not be managed properly. If you really want to have complete control over your cloud connected projects, the only way to go is to deploy your own server on the cloud.

This is exactly what we are going to do in this chapter. We are going to first create a cloud server so we can deploy web applications that can be accessed from anywhere. We are then going to discover how to deploy your own aREST cloud server on the server you just created. Finally, as a test, we'll connect a simple ESP8266 project to your own server. Let's start!

Hardware and software requirements

Let's first see what we need for this project. As we just want to test the connection between an ESP8266 board and your own cloud server, we'll keep things simple here.

For the ESP8266, I again chose to use an Adafruit ESP8266 module, along with an FTDI USB module.

We'll simply connect two kinds of component to this board: an LED and a DHT11 sensor.

Of course, you'll need the usual breadboard and jumper wires.

This is a list of all the components that will be used in this chapter:

- Adafruit ES8266 module (`https://www.adafruit.com/products/2471`)
- FTDI USB module (`https://www.adafruit.com/products/284`)
- LED (`https://www.sparkfun.com/products/9590`)
- 330 Ohm resistor (`https://www.sparkfun.com/products/8377`)
- DHT11 sensor (`https://www.adafruit.com/products/11`)
- Breadboard (`https://www.sparkfun.com/products/12002`)
- Jumper wires (`https://www.sparkfun.com/products/9194`)

On the software side, you will need the Arduino IDE and the aREST library, which we have already used earlier in the book. You will also need the PubSub library and the Adafruit DHT library.

Hardware configuration

We are now going to assemble the project. The hardware is really simple here, as we only want to test the connection between the project and our own cloud server we'll deploy later in this chapter.

Simply place the ESP8266 board on your breadboard, and then connect the FTDI breakout board to it.

For the LED, simply connect it in series with the resistor, with the longest pin of the LED connected to the resistor. Then, connect the remaining pin of the resistor to pin 5 of the ESP8266 board, and the remaining pin of the LED to the GND pin.

Once this is done, simply put the DHT11 sensor on the breadboard. Then, connect the left pin to VCC, the right pin to, and the pin next to VCC to pin 4 on your ESP8266 chip.

This is the final result:

Creating a cloud server

We are now going to take the first step towards having the board connected to your own cloud server: creating the server itself.

You could run the software we'll see later on your own computer, but then you won't be able to access your ESP8266 projects remotely. This is why you need to have your own server deployed with a cloud server provider. If you already have such a server capable of running the Meteor application (the framework we are going to use), you can just skip this section.

There are many server providers out there, but the one I recommend is Digital Ocean. They are fast, cheap, and have a very easy-to-use interface. You can find them at:

```
https://www.digitalocean.com/
```

Once you are on their website, create a new account. Then, create a new **Droplet**, which is the name for a server on Digital Ocean. You will be invited to choose where you want to deploy your Droplet (choose whatever is closest to the devices you want to use):

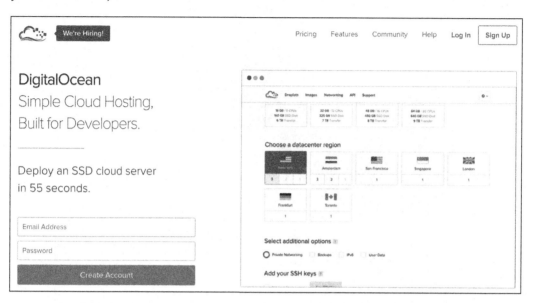

Next, you need to select your monthly plan, which will also determine the computing power of your server. As we only have a lightweight software here, the cheapest plan is more than enough for our server:

Next, you need to choose an operating system for your server. Simply choose the latest stable version of the Ubuntu Linux operating system:

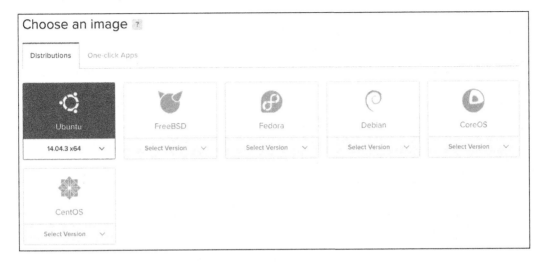

Finally, complete the creation of your server by giving it a name:

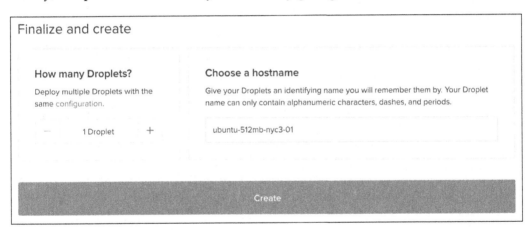

You should now see that your server has been created, and it should appear in the list:

From there, what you will need is the IP address of your server, which we are going to use later on.

You will also need to set root access on your server. As it's a complex process, I recommend following all the instructions here:

```
https://www.digitalocean.com/community/tutorials/how-to-configure-
ssh-key-based-authentication-on-a-linux-server
```

The aREST cloud server code

It's now time to actually deploy an application on the server that you just created. As the software for your cloud server, we are going to use the aREST cloud server that we have already used before.

It is completely free and open source, and you can get the latest version of the software from here:

```
https://github.com/marcoschwartz/meteor-aREST-mqtt
```

For now, simply copy all the files from this repository and put them inside any folder on your computer.

> This application actually uses the Meteor framework, which is a complete framework based on JavaScript and Node.js and can be used to create powerful web applications.
>
> If it's not been done yet, install Meteor on your computer by going to:
>
> https://www.meteor.com/install

Now, let's have a quick overview of the code of the aREST cloud server. The code is quite complicated, but I just wanted to highlight some parts here so you understand how it works.

Whenever a device connects to the server, the software first checks whether the server already knows the device. If that's the case, we set the device to connected, so it can be accessible from the cloud. If the device is unknown, it is added to the database on the server.

This is the piece of code that handles those functions:

```
Server.on('clientConnected', Meteor.bindEnvironment(function(client) {

    console.log('client connected', client.id);
```

```
   // Already exist?
   if (Devices.find({clientId: client.id}).fetch().length == 0) {

     // Insert in DB
     console.log('New device detected');
     device = {
       clientId: client.id,
       connected: true
     }
     Devices.insert(device);
   }
   else {
     console.log('Existing device detected');

     // Update device status
     Devices.update({clientId: client.id}, {$set: {"connected":
 true}});

   }

 }) );
```

Whenever the user wants to access a device, the user types a command inside a web browser. The cloud server will then first match this command with the commands that are available, for example:

```
Router.route('/:device', {
```

The server then checks whether the device exists:

```
var currentDevice = Devices.findOne({clientId: device});
```

If the device exists and is connected at the moment, the server prepares a message to be sent to the device, for example:

```
var message = {
  topic: currentDevice.clientId + '_in',
  payload: '',
  qos: 0,
  retain: false
};
```

Then, once the answer comes back from the device, we send it back to the user in JSON format:

```
answer = sendMessage(message);
this.response.setHeader('Content-Type', 'application/json');
this.response.end(answer);
```

Deploying the server

We are now going to deploy this software on your cloud server. First, you need to install Node.js if that's not been done yet. To do it, simply follow the instructions at:

```
https://nodejs.org/en/
```

We can then install some software called **Meteor Up**, which will really simplify the process of deploying the application on our web server.

Go to a terminal and type:

```
sudo npm install -g mup
```

Next, navigate to the folder in which you put all the files of the application, and initialize Meteor Up with:

```
mup init
```

This will create a file called `mup.json` inside the folder you are currently in. This is how this file will look:

```
{
  // Server authentication info
  "servers": [
    {
      "host": "0.0.0.0",
      "username": "root",
      //"password": "password"
      // or pem file (ssh based authentication)
      "pem": "~/.ssh/id_rsa"
    }
  ],

  // Install MongoDB in the server, does not destroy local MongoDB on
future setup
  "setupMongo": true,
```

```
    // WARNING: Node.js is required! Only skip if you already have Node.
js installed on server.
    "setupNode": true,

    // WARNING: If nodeVersion omitted will setup 0.10.36 by default. Do
not use v, only version number.
    "nodeVersion": "0.10.41",

    // Install PhantomJS in the server
    "setupPhantom": true,

    // Show a progress bar during the upload of the bundle to the
server.
    // Might cause an error in some rare cases if set to true, for
instance in Shippable CI
    "enableUploadProgressBar": true,

    // Application name (No spaces)
    "appName": "arest",

    // Location of app (local directory)
    "app": ".",

    // Configure environment
    "env": {
      "ROOT_URL": "http://localhost",
      "PORT": 3000
    },

    // Meteor Up checks if the app comes online just after the
deployment
    // before mup checks that, it will wait for no. of seconds
configured below
    "deployCheckWaitTime": 120
}
```

There are two things you will need to change in this file. The first one is to set the IP address of your Digital Ocean server:

```
"servers": [
    {
      "host": "0.0.0.0",
      "username": "root",
```

```
       //"password": "password"
       // or pem file (ssh based authentication)
       "pem": "~/.ssh/id_rsa"
    }
  ]
```

You can also change the port on which you want the application to run on your server. By default, it will be 3000, but you can change it in case you have several applications running on the same server:

```
"env": {
    "ROOT_URL": "http://localhost",
    "PORT": 3000
  }
```

Once that's done, save the file and type the following command:

```
mup setup
```

This will initialize your server so the Meteor application can be deployed:

Once you see the last **SUCCESS** message, you can continue and deploy the application with:

```
mup deploy
```

This will launch the deployment process:

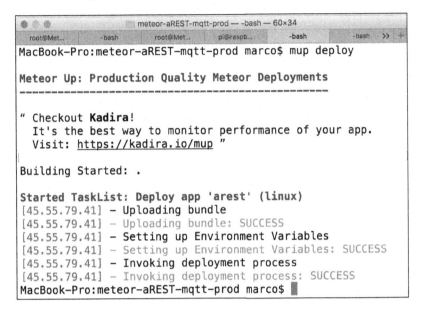

Once you see the final **SUCCESS** message in green, congratulations, you now have your own cloud server deployed, and ready to be used to control your IoT devices!

Connecting the ESP8266 board to your cloud server

We now actually want to test the server that we just deployed on the cloud. To do so, we are going to see how to configure the hardware we built earlier so it can connect to your own cloud server:

1. First, we need to include all the required libraries:

```
#include <ESP8266WiFi.h>
#include <PubSubClient.h>
#include <aREST.h>
#include "DHT.h"
```

2. Next, we define which pin the DHT sensor is connected to:

```
#define DHTPIN 4
#define DHTTYPE DHT11
```

3. Next, we create an instance of the DHT sensor:

```
DHT dht(DHTPIN, DHTTYPE, 15);
```

4. After that, we create clients to connect to your cloud server:

```
WiFiClient espClient;
PubSubClient client(espClient);
```

5. Next, we create the aREST instance. This is where you need to pass the IP address of your remote cloud server as an argument:

```
aREST rest = aREST(client, "192.168.0.103");
```

6. You also need to give an ID to your current device:

```
char* device_id = "01e47f";
```

7. Next, set the Wi-Fi name and password of the sketch:

```
const char* ssid = "wifi-name";
const char* password = "wifi-pass";
```

8. We also create two variables to hold the value of the measurements we are making:

```
float temperature;
float humidity;
```

9. In the setup() function of the sketch, we initialize the DHT sensor:

```
dht.begin();
```

10. We also expose the two measurement variables to the aREST API:

```
rest.variable("temperature", &temperature);
rest.variable("humidity", &humidity);
```

11. In the loop() function of the sketch, we measure the data coming from the sensor, and also keep the connection with your cloud server open:

```
// Reading temperature and humidity
humidity = dht.readHumidity();

// Read temperature as Celsius
temperature = dht.readTemperature();

// Connect to the cloud
rest.handle(client);
```

It's now time to test the sketch and see whether it can connect to the cloud server we just deployed! To check if that's the case, grab the code from the GitHub repository for the book. Then, modify the Wi-Fi name and password inside the code and upload it to the board.

Then, open the Serial monitor to check whether the connection to your cloud server can be established:

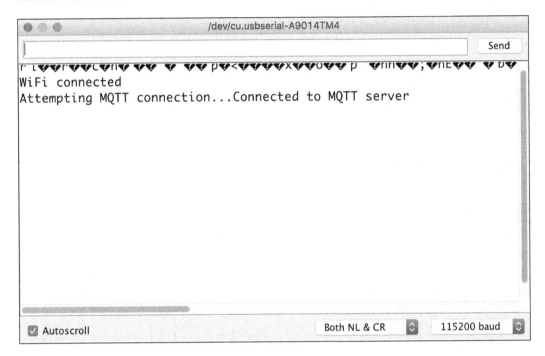

If you can see **Connected to MQTT server**, it means that your device is currently connected to the server you deployed in the cloud earlier, and the device is communicating via the aREST server, using the MQTT protocol. If not, go back to the process we saw in this chapter and make sure that the aREST application is correctly deployed on your cloud server.

You can now actually test the communication between your device and your cloud server, just as you did before with the aREST.io server. For example, to get the temperature, type:

```
http://19.434.34.23/01e47f/temperature
```

Of course, you need to replace the IP address with the one for your cloud server. You should immediately see the answer inside your web browser:

```
    {
"temperature": 26.00,
"id": "01e47f",
"name": "own_cloud",
"connected": true
    }
```

You can also set pin 5 as an output with:

```
http://19.434.34.23/01e47f/mode/5/o
```

Then, switch the LED on with:

```
http://19.434.34.23/01e47f/digital/5/1
```

Congratulations, you can now connect devices to your own cloud server!

Summary

In this chapter, we saw how to deploy your own server on the cloud, so you can have complete control over your Internet of Things projects with the ESP8266 Wi-Fi chip. We saw how to create your own server using Digital Ocean, how to deploy the aREST software there, and finally how to connect one ESP8266 to this newly deployed server.

You can of course now connect any of your ESP8266 projects to this server. You can simply use the projects you saw in this book that use aREST and connect them to your own server. You can also tinker with the code, and create new functions for your server application. If that's the case, don't hesitate to share your new features with the community!

Index

D

dashboard
cloud-based home automation system, controlling from 154-159
cloud-controlled ESP8266 robot, controlling from 188, 189

dashboard.arest.io
URL 146

data
displaying, Freeboard.io used 31
displaying, using Freeboard.io 32-35
logging, to Dweet.io 30, 31
reading, from digital sensor 20-23
reading, from GPIO pin 17
sending, via text message 99-102

DHT11 sensor
reference link 20

DHT library
URL 26

Digital Ocean
URL 193
URL, for tutorials 196

digital sensor
data, reading from 21-23

door lock, controlling with ESP8266 Wi-Fi chip
about 109
ESP8266 board, configuring 112, 113
from cloud 113, 114
hardware, configuring 111
notifications, receiving when lock is opened 114-119

Dweet.io
data, logging 30, 31

E

e-mail notifications
Adafruit ES8266 module, URL 90
Breadboard, URL 90
DHT11 sensor, URL 90
FTDI USB module, URL 90
hardware configuration 91
Jumper wires, URL 90
sending 91-99

e-mail notifications,
sending with ESP8266 chip 89

ESP8266 board
connecting, to custom cloud server 201-204

ESP8266 chip
Facebook post, creating from 62-69

ESP8266 module
about 1-3
Arduino IDE, installing 10
configuring 39-43
connecting, to WiFi network 11, 12
details, reference link 3
selecting 1-3
URL 2

F

Facebook post
creating, from ESP8266 chip 62-69

Freeboard.io
URL 32
used, for displaying data 31-34

G

GPIO pin
data, reading from 17

H

hardware configuration,
for ESP8266 board 26-28

hardware requisites,
e-mail notifications 89, 90

hardware requisites, ESP8266
3.3V FTDI USB module 6
about 4, 5, 25, 26
Breadboard 6
breadboard 3.3V power supply 6
hardware configuration 7-9
jumper wires 6
olimex module 6

hardware requisites, for cloud data logging
3.3V FTDI USB module, URL 26
Breadboard 3.3V power supply, URL 26
DHT11 sensor, URL 26

CPSIA information can be obtained
at www.ICGtesting.com
Printed in the USA
BVOW10s0028291116

469129BV00009B/56/P